CW01546596

Mini Rice Cooker Cookbook

110 Delicious Recipes for Your Mini Rice Cooker for Everybody

Amiyah Reyes

TABLE OF CONTENT

INTRODUCTION:

Welcome to the enticing world of the "Mini Rice Cooker Cookbook: 110 Delicious Recipes for Your Mini Rice Cooker for Everybody" by Amiyah Reyes. This cookbook is a culinary treasure trove designed to revolutionize your cooking experience with the humble yet versatile mini rice cooker.

In our fast-paced lives, convenience in the kitchen is essential, and the mini rice cooker emerges as a compact powerhouse, ready to whip up delectable dishes with minimal effort. Whether you're a busy professional, a college student, or simply someone looking to streamline your cooking routine, this cookbook is tailored just for you.

Amiyah Reyes, the creative mind behind this collection, is passionate about transforming everyday ingredients into extraordinary meals. With 110 carefully curated recipes, she invites you on a culinary journey spanning breakfast, side dishes, soups, stews, beef, pork, chicken, poultry, fish, seafood, and one-pot rice meals. Each recipe is crafted to showcase the versatility and efficiency of your mini rice cooker, making it an indispensable tool in your kitchen.

Discover the joy of waking up to mouthwatering breakfasts, explore innovative side dishes to elevate your meals, and savor the rich flavors of hearty soups and stews. From succulent beef and pork dishes to wholesome chicken and poultry options and delightful fish and seafood creations, this cookbook ensures diverse culinary experiences. The one-pot rice meals section adds a touch of simplicity to your cooking routine, promising delicious and hassle-free meals in a single pot.

Whether you are a novice in the kitchen or an experienced home chef, the "Mini Rice Cooker Cookbook" offers something for everyone. Each recipe is accompanied by clear instructions, helpful tips, and a dash of culinary inspiration, empowering you to make the most of your mini rice cooker.

Prepare to embark on a culinary adventure that will save you time and tantalize your taste buds with various flavors and textures. Join Amiyah Reyes in unlocking the full potential of your mini rice cooker and revolutionizing your cooking experience—one delicious recipe at a time. Enjoy the simplicity, convenience, and culinary delight the mini rice cooker brings your kitchen.

Happy cooking!

1. Breakfast:

Start your day on a delicious note with various breakfast recipes designed for your mini rice cooker. From classic Rice Cooker Rice Pudding to innovative Breakfast Burritos with Cilantro Lime Cauliflower Rice and even Soft and fluffy Rice Cooker Bread, this chapter has something to suit every morning mood.

2. Side Dish:

Enhance your meals with flavorful side dishes that are easy to prepare in your mini rice cooker. Indulge in Parmesan Risotto, Easy Spanish Rice, Sushi Rice, and more. This chapter is a collection of versatile and mouthwatering accompaniments, from simple Basmati Rice to exotic Coconut Rice.

3. Soup & Stew:

Warm up with comforting soups and stews crafted effortlessly in your rice cooker. Explore recipes like Carrot Ginger Soup, Rice-Cooker Thai Chicken Noodle Soup, and Taco Soup in the Rice Cooker for a satisfying and hearty dining experience.

4. Beef & Pork:

Savor the richness of beef and pork dishes cooked to perfection in your mini rice cooker. From the savory Black Pepper Beef and Broccoli Fried Rice to the sweet Pineapple Pork Fried Rice, this chapter offers a delightful array of options, including classics like Mushroom Risotto and Sweet and Sour Pork with Rice.

5. Main Dishes:

Elevate your main course with a diverse selection of dishes that showcase the versatility of your mini rice cooker. Try the vibrant Rainbow Fried Rice, the fragrant Thai Strawberry Sticky Rice, or the comforting Five Spice Chicken. This chapter is a culinary journey through myriad flavors, textures, and international cuisines.

6. Chicken & Poultry:

Discover the ease of preparing chicken and poultry dishes in your mini rice cooker. From the aromatic Rice Cooker Chicken and Sausage Jambalaya to the creamy Cajun Chicken Pasta, these recipes ensure that your chicken and poultry dishes are flavorful and convenient.

7. Fish & Seafood:

Dive into a sea of flavors with fish and seafood recipes that are a breeze to cook in your mini rice cooker. Enjoy the simplicity of Lemon Dill Rice, the richness of Spicy Tuna Sushi Bowl with Crispy Rice, and the exotic flavors of Paella—all prepared easily in your rice cooker.

8. One Pot Rice Meals:

Streamline your cooking process with one-pot rice meals that combine protein, vegetables, and grains in a single pot. Explore the Pineapple Teriyaki, Hainanese Chicken Rice, and other creative recipes that make cooking and cleaning up a breeze.

9. Dessert & Cake:

Indulge your sweet tooth with tempting dessert and cake recipes made right in your mini rice cooker. This chapter is a sweet finale to your culinary adventure, from classic Rice Pudding to the delightful Rice Cooker Japanese Cheesecake and the decadent Chocolate Cake.

Embark on a culinary journey with Amiyah Reyes as your guide, and let the "Mini Rice Cooker Cookbook" transform your kitchen into a hub of delicious and convenient creations. Happy cooking!

The choice between a mini rice cooker and a normal (standard-sized) rice cooker depends on your specific needs, kitchen space, and the quantity of rice you typically prepare. Here are some factors to consider when comparing the two:

Capacity:

The most apparent difference is the capacity. Mini rice cookers are designed for smaller servings, typically 1 to 3 cups of uncooked rice. Standard rice cookers come in various sizes, accommodating larger quantities, such as 5 to 10 cups or more. Choose the size that aligns with your regular rice consumption.

Kitchen Space:

Mini rice cookers are compact and ideal for kitchens with limited counter or storage space. A mini rice cooker might be a practical choice if your kitchen is small or has minimal storage. On the other hand, standard rice cookers may require more counter space or storage room.

Portability:

Mini rice cookers are often more portable and suitable for those who travel frequently or have limited kitchen facilities. They are convenient for small apartments, dorm rooms, or offices. Standard rice cookers are generally less portable due to their larger size.

Versatility:

Standard rice cookers often come with more features and cooking options. They may include settings for different types of rice, steaming functions, and programmable timers. Mini rice cookers may have simpler functionalities but can still cook basic rice dishes.

Cooking Time:

Mini rice cookers tend to have shorter cooking times since they are designed for smaller quantities. A standard rice cooker may be more time-efficient if you need to prepare large batches of rice regularly.

Cost:

Generally, mini rice cookers are more affordable than their larger counterparts. A mini rice cooker might be a cost-effective choice if you're on a budget and typically cook smaller portions.

Energy Efficiency:

Mini rice cookers use less energy compared to larger ones. If you're conscious about energy consumption or have a small household, a mini rice cooker might be a more environmentally friendly option.

Multifunctionality:

Some standard rice cookers have additional functions like slow cooking, sautéing, or baking. A standard rice cooker may be a better fit if you're looking for a versatile appliance that can handle various cooking tasks.

In summary, choosing between a mini rice cooker and a normal-sized rice cooker depends on your lifestyle, kitchen space, and cooking needs. A mini rice cooker might be the right choice if you typically cook small portions and have limited space. If you often cook for a larger group and have the space for it, a standard-sized rice cooker with more features could be a better fit.

1. RICE COOKER RICE PUDDING

Prep Time: 5 Minutes | Cook Time: 1 hour | Cooking Time: 20 Minutes

Total Time: 1 Hour 25 Minutes | Serving: 4 Cups

Ingredients

- ½ cup of long grain rice I use Jasmine.
- ¼ tsp kosher salt
- 3 cups of milk
- 1 cup of water
- ¼ cup of sugar

Instructions

1. After rinsing, drain the rice.
2. Cook on the rice setting after adding the rice and water to the rice cooker.
3. Mix thoroughly after adding the milk, sugar, and salt to the rice. Specify the porridge setting for cooking.
4. If you lack a porridge setting, select "cook," leave the lid open, and cook for 45 to 50 minutes.
5. Stir the rice once more and thoroughly mix it until it thickens and takes on the consistency of pudding. Turn the heat back to the porridge setting and cook for 10 to 15 minutes or until the consistency reaches your desired level.
6. Serve and savor with your preferred garnishes, such as chopped almonds for crunch, dried raisins, berries for an excellent taste, and a sprinkle of cinnamon!

2. RICE COOKER CONGEE

Prep Time: 10 Minutes | Cook Time: 50 Minutes

Total Time: 1 Hour | Serving: 3

Ingredients

- 14 ounce (1) can chicken broth
- ¼ tsp kosher salt
- 1 tbsp size piece of ginger, peeled
- ¼ cup of rice (short or long grain) use US measuring cup (liquid or dry)
- ½ cup of chicken, cut into bite sized pieces
- 3 cups of water
- 1 clove garlic, smashed

Garnish and add ons:

- cracked pepper
- chil sauce I like Sambal Oelek brand
- squeeze of lime
- sliced green onions
- Chinese donut
- fried shallots

Instructions

1. Use a mesh strainer to wash the rice. Be sure to shake it well to get rid of any extra water.
2. Put the chicken broth, water, rice, garlic, ginger, chicken, and kosher salt in the pot. Combine the things in a bowl.
3. On the oatmeal setting, press "cook." Leave the lid off and set it to cook if it doesn't have a porridge setting. Cook for 45 to 50 minutes.
4. Add green onions and cracked pepper to the top, or use any other toppings and sides you like.

3. APPLE CINNAMON STEEL CUT OATMEAL

Prep Time: 5 Minutes | Cook Time: 10 Minutes

Total Time:45 Minutes | Serving: 4

Ingredients

- ♦ Butter
- ♦ Brown sugar
- ♦ 1 cup of milk
- ♦ 1 Granny Smith apple, small diced
- ♦ 1 tsp. cinnamon
- ♦ 1 cup of water
- ♦ 1 cup of steel cut oatmeal
- ♦ Cream, optional

Instructions

1. Add oatmeal, water, milk, apples, and cinnamon using a rice cooker. Stir the ingredients together. Follow the maker's directions and cook for 30 to 40 minutes on the whole grain rice setting. Brown sugar and butter should be added before serving. Cream is not required but is tasty.

4. WHOLE-GRAIN BREAKFAST PORRIDGE

Prep Time: 15 Minutes | Cook Time: 55 Minutes | Inactive Time: 6 Hors

Total Time: 7 Hours 10 Minutes | Serving: 4

Ingredients

- 1/2 cup of steel-cut oats
- 1/2 cup of red or wild rice
- 1 2-inch piece orange peel
- 1 to 2 tbsp packed dark or light brown sugar
- 1 cinnamon stick
- 1/2 cup of farina or wheat cereal
- 1/4 cup of dried fruit (cranberries, cherries, raisins and/or chopped apricots)
- 1/4 cup of pearl barley or farro
- 1/4 tsp salt
- Chopped nuts, maple syrup and/or milk, for serving (optional)

Instructions

1. Put the barley, rice, oats, and farina in a 6- to 10-cup rice cooker up to 12 hours before you want to serve. Sugar, salt, 5 cups of water, and the orange peel should all be mixed. Put the dried fruit in.
2. Put the pot away, set the timer, and program it for the porridge cycle. That way, breakfast will be ready when you want it to be. Setting your rice cooker for 50 to 55 minutes should work if it has no porridge setting.
3. You can serve the warm porridge with nuts, syrup, and milk.

5. RICE COOKER WHEAT BERRIES

Prep Time: 5 Minutes | Cook Time: 45 Minutes

Total Time: 50 Minutes | Serving: 4

Ingredients

- ◆ 1 cup of dry wheat berries
- ◆ 2-2½ cups of water

Instructions

1. Before cooking, rinse your wheat berries to remove dust and extra starch. Spray cooking spray on the bottom of the bowl of your rice cooker to keep things from sticking.
2. Put water and wheat berries in the bowl of the rice cooker. How chewy do you want your wheat berries to affect the amount of grain to water? For every cup of wheat berries, add 2 cups of water if you like them chewy. You can add 2.5 cups of water for every cup of wheat berries if you want them to be softer.
3. Make the rice, then sit back and wait. While every rice cooker is different, it takes about 45 minutes to cook 1 cup of wheat berries. Fork-fluff the rice when it's done cooking, and then eat it however you like!

6. RICE COOKER FRITTATA

Prep Time: 10 Minutes | Cook Time: 15 Minutes

Total Time: 25 Minutes | Serving: 2

Ingredients

♦ 3-4 eggs (more if you're cooking for a family)
♦ 1/2 cup of cheese
♦ Salt and pepper to taste
♦ 1 cup of vegetables (chopped or sliced)
♦ Chopped or diced meat (optional)

Instructions

1. Spray cooking spray that doesn't stick inside the rice cooker.
2. Fry the eggs in a medium-sized bowl.
3. Mix the vegetables (and meat, if you want).
4. Use salt and pepper to suit your taste.
5. Put the whole thing into the rice cooker.
6. Cover the whole thing with cheese.
7. Press the "cook" button and put the lid back on the rice cooker.
8. For about 15 minutes, or until the eggs are set, cook the frittata.
9. Use a plastic spatula to carefully take the frittata out of the pan when it's done and place it on a plate. Serve it with toast and fruit after cutting it up.

7. RICE COOKER CHEESY GRITS

Prep Time: 10 Minutes | Cook Time: 30 Minutes

Total Time: 40 Minutes | Serving: 2

Ingredients

- 4 cups of water
- pinch of salt
- 2 tbsp butter
- 1 cup of yellow grits
- 1/2 cup of asiago or cheddar cheese
- 1/4 cup of heavy cream

Instructions

1. I use a rice cooker to make the grits. I add a little salt to the grits, water, and rice cooker and press the button.
2. You can add extra pepper and salt to taste after cooking the grits. Then, mix in the cheese, butter, and heavy cream. Use the rice cooker or the pan to keep the grits warm.

8. BREAKFAST BURRITOS WITH CILANTRO LIME

Prep Time: 10 Minutes | Cook Time: 25 Minutes

Total Time: 35 Minutes | Serving: 6

Ingredients

- 6 eggs
- 4 ounce diced green chiles, canned
- 5 cups of cauliflower rice
- 1 tsp chili lime seasoning
- 1 tsp cumin
- 1/4 cup of fresh cilantro, chopped
- 2 cups of fat free cheddar cheese
- 6 low carb wraps, I used: Toufayan brand
- 3/4 cup of fat free refried beans
- 1 tsp onion powder
- 1/2 tsp kosher salt
- 1 tsp garlic powder
- 1/4 cup of lime juice
- 1 tsp kosher salt
- 1 cup of egg whites
- 1 cup of onion, chopped

Instructions

1. Cut the onion up. Set a frying pan on medium heat to get it hot.
2. With 1/2 tsp kosher salt, add olive oil spray and cook the onion for 5 minutes.
3. After adding the diced green chiles, it will take another 5 minutes to cook.
4. Whisk the egg whites and yolks in a bowl.
5. Put the eggs in the pan and season them with chili lime, onion powder, and garlic powder.
6. Add the cheddar cheese and mix it in after cooking the eggs all the way through.
7. The eggs ought to be taken out of the pan and set aside.
8. Spray more olive oil spray on the pan after wiping it clean.
9. Use the microwave to thaw the cauliflower rice.
10. Now, add the cauliflower rice to the pan. Cook for 10 minutes until there is no more water in the rice and some spots turn brown.
11. Put aside the cilantro, cumin, lime juice, and one tsp of kosher salt.
12. Spread two tbsp of the refried beans on each tortilla to get them ready. Then add 3/4 cup of the cauliflower rice and the egg mixture.
13. Place a tortilla on a piece of foil and roll it up tight. Then, wrap the tortilla in the foil and roll it up tight again.

9. SOFT & FLUFFY RICE COOKER BREAD

Prep Time: 10 Minutes | Cook Time: 35 Minutes

Total Time: 45 Minutes | Serving: 6

Ingredients

- 40g cake flour
- 1 tsp instant yeast (3g)
- 1/4 tsp salt
- 1/2 cup + 1 tbsp lukewarm oat milk (136ml // or soy milk)
- 2 tsp vegan butter or margarine (10g)
- 160g bread flour
- 1 1/2 tbsp organic cane sugar (22g)

Instructions

1. Add the sugar, yeast, oat milk, vegan butter, bread flour, and cake flour to a stand mix. For 30 seconds, knead at a low speed (setting #2). Then, for 5 minutes, knead at a medium-high speed (setting #4). When you use a bowl, do the same thing, but for 10 minutes, knead the dough with your hands.
2. Make a ball out of it and put it in the rice cooker. Set to 10 minutes to stay warm. After 30 minutes, or when the dough is 1.5 inches thick, turn off the "keep warm" setting and let it ferment.
3. Make a log of the dough by punching it down and kneading it a few times. Cut the dough into six equal pieces. Make small balls out of it again by kneading it. Put it in the rice cooker and set it to 10 minutes on "keep warm." Finally, turn off the "keep warm" setting. Let the dough proof for another 20 to 30 minutes or until it grows to x1.5 size. Because each rice cooker is different, do a poke test to be sure. If you poke the dough, it should slowly spring back. It moves too quickly and needs more time. What if it doesn't spring back? It has been fermented too long. After the dough has been proofed, cook it in quick mode. When it's done, turn the bread over and cook it again on quick mode. The bread is ready when the second cycle is over.

10. PULL-APART PIZZA BREAD IN A RICE COOKER

Prep Time: 20 Minutes | Cook Time: 2 Hour

Total Time: 2 Hour 20 Minutes | Serving: 9

Ingredients

- pepperoni
- grated parmesan
- dried oregano
- mozzarella cheese
- olive oil
- pre-made biscuit dough
- marinara sauce for dipping

Instructions

1. Put pepperoni and mozzarella cheese inside a round of biscuit dough, then seal the dough.
2. Spread olive oil on each biscuit ball and then top each one with dried oregano and Parmesan.

11. PARMESAN RISOTTO RICE COOKER RECIPE

Prep Time: 15 Minutes | Cook Time: 1 Hour 15 Minutes

Total Time: 1 Hour 30 Minutes | Serving: 4

Ingredients

- 1 2/3 Cups of chicken broth
- Salt and pepper
- ½ tsp minced garlic
- 3 Tbsp butter
- 1 Cups of arborio rice or other risotto rice
- ¼ Cups of chopped onion
- 2 Tbsp extra butter
- 3 Tbsp freshly grated parmesan cheese

Instructions

1. To cook the rice, use two tbsp of butter, onion, and garlic.
2. It's time to cook the rice. After the butter melts, let it "cook" for two more minutes.
3. Combine in the arborio rice and cook for 10 minutes, until the rice is mostly clear but has a small white spot in the middle of each grain.
4. Add the salt, broth, and pepper, stir, and put the lid back on. Start the timer again. It will take longer to cook than usual because there is so much liquid, so give yourself extra time.
5. After the machine is done, let it sit for at least 10 minutes or until you're ready to serve. Then, add the last tbsp of butter and the parmesan cheese and mix again.

12. EASY SPANISH RICE RECIPE

Prep Time: 5 Minutes | Cook Time: 30 Minutes

Total Time: 35 Minutes | Serving: 5 cups

Ingredients

- ½ tsp garlic powder
- 3 ½ cups of water
- 2 cups of white rice
- 1-3 tbsp chili powder
- 1 small onion diced
- 1 tsp cumin or smoked cumin
- 3 bouillon cubes or 3 tsp Better than Bouillon
- 1 tsp salt
- 1 can diced tomatoes with juice (14-ounce)

Instructions

1. Put the rice in the bottom of the rice cooker. Next, add the water and diced tomatoes. For the spices to mix with the water, add the onion and spices and stir them around a bit on top.
2. Follow the manufacturer's directions when cooking.
3. Taste the rice to see if it needs more salt after cooking.
4. It can be a side dish or put inside your favorite tacos and burritos.

13. BASMATI RICE IN A RICE COOKER

Prep Time: 5 Minutes | Cook Time: 15 Minutes

Total Time: 20 Minutes | Serving: 3

Ingredients

- Salt to taste
- 1 cup of basmati rice
- 1 ¾ cups of water

Instructions

1. Run cold water over the basmati rice several times to clean it well. This helps remove extra starch and ensures the rice is cooked fluffy.
2. Place the rice that has been rinsed inside the rice cooker.
3. Add the water. One cup of basmati rice needs 1.75 cups of water, which is the general ratio. However, you can change the amount of water depending on how sticky or dry you like your rice.
4. Feel free to add salt. To begin, add about ½ tsp of salt and then change the amount to your liking.
5. Close the lid and put the inner pot inside the rice cooker.
6. Choose the "Cook" or "White Rice" setting on your rice cooker if it has those options. Set the timer for about 15 to 20 minutes if there is one. Most of the time, basmati rice cooks faster than other types.
7. Let the rice cooker cook all the way through. Once the rice is done, the rice cooker will switch to the "Keep Warm" setting on its own.
8. Close the lid and let the rice sit in the rice cooker for another 5 to 10 minutes. This enables the rice to steam and get even fluffier.
9. When the time is up, open the rice cooker and use a fork to gently fluff the rice to separate the grains.
10. Warm up the basmati rice and serve it as a side dish or a base for your favorite curries, stir-fries, or other foods.

14. SUSHI RICE IN A RICE COOKER

Prep Time: 5 Minutes | Cook Time: 30 Minutes

Total Time: 35 Minutes | Serving: 6

Ingredients

- ◆ 1.5 cups of sushi rice
- ◆ 1/4 cup of seasoned rice vinegar
- ◆ 2 cups of filtered water

Instructions

1. Put the rice and water in a rice cooker. Follow the cooker's "white rice" setting to cook the rice.
2. If you want to season the vinegar, do it over the cooked grains when the rice is done. Be gentle as you toss everything around to spread the vinegar even more. If you mash the grains, they will get sticky.
3. It's now ready to be used for sushi.

15. CILANTRO LIME RICE

Prep Time: 10 Minutes | Cook Time: 20 Minutes

Total Time: 30 Minutes | Serving: 8

Ingredients

- ◆ 1 lime, zested
- ◆ 2 tbsp minced fresh cilantro
- ◆ 2 tbsp lime juice, freshly squeezed
- ◆ 1 tsp kosher salt
- ◆ 1 tsp light olive oil
- ◆ 2 cups of long grain white rice

Instructions

1. For 10 inches, heat the pan over medium to low heat. Add the rice and oil. Stir the rice and toast it for 5-8 minutes or until it turns golden and smells good.
2. Toast the rice and add salt to the rice cooker. Follow the manufacturer's instructions to fill the container to the proper water level (for me, that's 2 inches), then put the lid on and start cooking.
3. Open the rice cooker and use a fork to fluff the rice when it's done. After that, put it in a bowl and add the lime juice, zest, and cilantro. You can taste it and add more cilantro, zest, or juice if you want.

16. FRIED RICE

Prep Time: 5 Minutes | Cook Time: 10 Minutes

Total Time: 15 Minutes | Serving: 4-6

Ingredients

- salt and black pepper
- 4 cups of cooked and chilled rice
- 3 cloves garlic, minced
- 3 tbsp butter, divided
- 1/2 tsp toasted sesame oil
- 3 green onions, thinly sliced
- 1 small white onion, diced
- 2 large eggs, whisked
- 2 medium carrots, peeled and diced
- 1/2 cup of frozen peas
- 2 tsp oyster sauce (optional)
- 3–4 tbsp soy sauce, or more to taste

Instructions

1. Add 1/2 tbsp of butter in a large saute pan and melt it over medium-high heat. When you add the egg, stir it to make it scrambled. Take the egg out and put it on a different plate.
2. Add one more tbsp to the pan to make the butter melt and heat it up. Season with pepper and salt, then put the carrots, onion, peas, and garlic. The carrots and onion should be soft after about 5 minutes of cooking. Switch the heat to high, add the last 1 1/2 tbsp of butter, and mix until it melts. Add the rice, green onions, soy sauce, and oyster sauce (if used) immediately and mix them. Keep sauteing for three more minutes, stirring now and then, to fry the rice. (Before stirring, I like to break the rice so the bottom can get crispy.) Then add the eggs and mix everything. Take it off the heat and mix in the sesame oil until everything is well mixed. If you think it needs more salt, add more soy sauce.

17. EASY RICE COOKER GARLIC BUTTER RICE

Prep Time: 5 Minutes | Cook Time: 40 Minutes

Total 45Minutes | Serving: 4 cups

Ingredients

- ◆ 2 tsp garlic, minced about 2-3 cloves
- ◆ 1 cup of Jasmine rice use US measuring (dry) cup
- ◆ 1 ½ cup of chicken broth
- ◆ 2 tbsp Salted butter, cut in half pieces
- ◆ ½ tsp Kosher salt

Instructions

1. Make sure to wash and rinse the rice well.
2. Add rice, chicken broth, garlic, butter, and salt to the pot. Add the things and mix them well.
3. Use the white rice setting on the cooker to start cooking.
4. Use a small plastic spoon to fluff the rice when it's done, and serve!

18. QUINOA IN A RICE COOKER

Prep Time: 5 Minutes | Cook Time: 30 Minutes

Total Time: 35 Minutes | Serving: 6

Ingredients

- ◆ 1 cup of quinoa
- ◆ 2 cups of water or broth
- ◆ 1/2 tsp salt (optional)

Instructions

1. Rinse the quinoa. You can use broth or water to cook the quinoa. You could use water if you still determine what you will do with it. If you know what you want to do in the future, broth can be an excellent way to spice things up.
2. Put salt in the rice cooker and turn it on.That's how long it will take to cook most of them. As soon as it's done cooking, give it a quick stir with a fork.
3. About 3 to 4 cups of quinoa will be made.

19. RICE COOKER RICE AND BEANS

Prep Time: 5 Minutes | Cook Time: 25 Minutes

Total Time: 30 Minutes | Serving: 3

Ingredients

- Salt to taste
- 1/2 tsp cumin
- 1/2 tsp garlic powder
- 2 cups of water or vegetable broth
- 1 cup of white rice
- 1/2 tsp oregano
- 1 15ounce can black beans, drained and rinsed
- 1 bay leaf
- 1/2 tsp onion powder

Instructions

1. Put the uncooked rice, water, black beans, and spices in a rice cooker. Cover and stir.
2. Use the white rice setting to cook. If you use a rice cooker, it should take about 25 minutes.
3. Throw away the bay leaf after cooking the rice, fluff it with a fork, and add more seasonings to taste.

20. COCONUT RICE IN RICE COOKER

Prep Time: 20 Minutes | Cook Time: 30 Minutes | additional Time: 10 Minutes

Total Time: 60 Minutes | Serving: 8

Ingredients

- 1/2 cup of water or coconut water
- 1 can (14 ounce.) coconut milk
- 1 tsp salt
- 1/2 cup of shredded coconut (sweetened or unsweetened)
- 2 cups of (400 grams) Jasmine Rice

Instructions

1. Place the rice in the pot for the rice cooker and wash it in cold water until the water runs clear. This should take about three to four times. After you drain the rice, put it in cold water and let it soak for 15 minutes. Then, drain it.
2. Stir the rice together after adding the coconut milk, water, and salt.
3. Turn on the rice cooker and choose the "White Rice" setting. Then, put the rice pot inside the cooker and close the lid.
4. It will "Keep Warm" for about 30 minutes after the rice is done cooking.
5. Open the lid, add the shredded coconut, and fluff the rice by stirring it with a serving spatula to spread out any extra liquid.
6. You can serve it immediately, cover it, and keep it warm until you're ready to use it.

23. CILANTRO LIME QUINOA

Prep Time: 5 Minutes | Cook Time: 20 Minutes

Total Time: 25 Minutes | Serving: 1

Ingredients

- 2 tbsp fresh lime juice
- 2 cups of vegetable broth
- Salt and pepper to taste
- 1/3 cup of chopped cilantro
- 1 cup of quinoa rinsed and drained
- 1 clove garlic minced

Instructions

1. Put the broth and quinoa into a large pot. Bring up the temperature. Cover, fewer the heat, and cook for 15 minutes until the broth is gone and the quinoa is soft. Take it off the heat and cover it for 5 minutes. Take off the lid and use a fork to fluff up the quinoa.
2. It's time to add the cilantro, lime juice, and garlic. To taste, add salt and pepper. Warm up and serve.

24. RICE COOKER MEXICAN RICE

Prep Time: 10 Minutes | Cook Time: 5 Minutes

Total Time: 15 Minutes | Serving: 1

Ingredients

- Fresh black pepper
- Salt as needed
- 3 1/8 cup of low sodium chicken broth (use 1/4 to 1/3 cup of less liquid for drier rice)
- 3 Tbsp butter
- 1/2 cup of onion, finely diced
- 4.5 ounce. can tomato paste
- Pinch of red pepper flakes
- Cilantro for garnish
- 4 ounce. can diced green chilies
- 1 1/2 cups of long grain rice

Instructions

1. Put everything into the rice cooker. Mix well. Follow the manufacturer's directions when cooking. Do not stir for at least three minutes after cooking. This will help the sauce thicken. Add cilantro as a garnish before serving.

25. RICE COOKER PANCAKE

Prep Time: 5 Minutes | Cook Time: 50 Minutes

Total Time: 55 Minutes | Serving: 8

Ingredients

- 1/4 cup of unsalted butter , melted
- 2 cups of all-purpose flour , spooned and leveled
- 1/4 tsp cinnamon
- 1 tsp salt
- 1/3 cup of blueberries (fresh or frozen)
- 2 large eggs
- 1 & 1/2 cups of whole milk
- 2 tsp baking powder
- 1 tsp baking soda
- 1/4 cup of granulated sugar
- For serving: pat of butter, maple syrup, and blueberries

Instructions

1. Combine the baking soda, flour, salt, baking powder, sugar, and cinnamon in a large bowl with a whisk. Mix the eggs, milk, and melted butter with a whisk.
2. Sprinkle some flour on the blueberries, and then use a spatula to gently mix them into the batter until they are all mixed in.
3. Cover the bowl of your rice cooker with cooking spray that doesn't stick. Cover the bowl with the lid and set the rice cooker to cook or steam for 50 minutes.
4. Put it on a cutting board. Cut into eight wedges that are all the same size.
5. Please immediately put it on each plate and top it with a pat of butter, a drizzle of maple syrup, and some fresh blueberries.

26. CARROT GINGER SOUP IN RICE COOKER

Prep Time: 10 Minutes | Cook Time: 1 Hour 20 Minutes

Total Time: 1 Hour 30 Minutes | Serving: 4

Ingredients

- ◆ 3 cups of vegetable broth or water
- ◆ 2 tbsp grated ginger (3 tbsp for a spicier kick)
- ◆ Salt and pepper, as needed
- ◆ ½ cup of sour cream
- ◆ 1 pound carrots, peeled and chopped
- ◆ 1 tbsp fresh flat parsley, chopped
- ◆ 1 small onion, finely chopped

Instructions

1. Put the ginger, vegetable broth, chopped carrots, and onion into the inner pot of your rice cooker. Make sure that the ingredients are spread out evenly.
2. Turn your rice cooker to the "Slow Cook" setting. Put 75 minutes on the timer and press the "Start" button. From here, the cooker will do its thing.
3. Carefully move the cooked mixture to a blender when the timer goes off. Be careful with it because it will be hot.
4. Put ⅓ cup of sour cream into the blender. Put the lid back on and blend the ingredients until they are smooth. If you think it needs it, add salt and pepper.
5. To serve, pour the blended soup into bowls set aside for serving. For an extra flavor boost, sprinkle fresh parsley on top to finish.

27. RICE-COOKER THAI CHICKEN NOODLE SOUP

Prep Time: 10 Minutes | Cook Time: 1 Hour 15 Minutes

Total Time: 1 Hour 25 Minutes | Serving: 4

Ingredients

- 300g (10.5 ounce) fresh egg noodles (or noodles of your choice)
- 1 cup of bean shoots
- roughly chopped coriander (cilantro), to serve
- Thai chilli powder, to serve (optional)
- roughly chopped spring onion (scallions), to serve

Soup broth:

- 1 tsp sugar
- 1 tbsp sea salt
- 4cm (1.5 inch) piece ginger, sliced
- 6 garlic cloves
- 1 tsp black peppercorns
- 6 coriander (cilantro) roots
- 1 tbsp fish sauce
- 2 litres (2.1 qt) chicken stock
- 2 chicken Marylands

Chilli vinegar:

- ⅓ cup of white vinegar
- 1 long red chilli, thinly sliced

Instructions

1. A mortar and pestle can make a rough paste of garlic, coriander roots, and peppercorns. Put this in the rice cooker basket with the Maryland chicken, ginger, fish sauce, sugar, and salt. Add the chicken stock. Put the lid back on and choose the SOUP setting. Leave the chicken to cook for an hour or until it is fully cooked.
2. For the chili vinegar, put the vinegar and chili in a small bowl and set it aside.
3. Use tongs to get the chicken out of the rice cooker bowl and into a bowl. When the chicken is cool enough to handle, shred it and throw away the bones. Pour the soup broth through a sieve into a large bowl or pot. Put the broth back into the clean rice cooker bowl if you want to use the KEEP WARM setting.
4. To cook the noodles, put 6 cups of water in the rice cooker and set it to the SOUP function. Then, heat the water until it starts to simmer. After adding the noodles, cook them according to the steps on the package until they are tender. Take the noodles out of the water and put them in bowls to serve.
5. Add the chicken shreds, coriander, and spring onions to the noodles. Put the soup on top of it. Add bean shoots on top and serve with chili vinegar and Thai chili powder if you want to use it.

28. DAIKON AND CHICKEN SOUP

Prep Time: 30 Minutes | Cook Time: 1 Hour

Total Time: 1 Hour 30 Minutes | Serving: 4

Ingredients

- 1 tsp sugar
- 1 free range chicken (Indonesian: ayam kampung), cut into 4-8 pieces
- 2 inches ginger, peeled and bruised
- 3 cloves garlic, minced
- 2 stalks scallion, thinly sliced
- 2 stalks celery, thinly sliced, reserve the leaves for garnish
- 1 daikon, peeled and cut into sticks
- ½ onion, finely chopped
- 1 liter water
- 2 tsp salt

Instructions

1. In a pot, boil the daikon for 10 minutes. Then, drain it and set it aside.
2. Warm up two tbsp of oil in a pot. Fry the garlic and onion for 2 to 3 minutes until they smell good. Place the chicken pieces and garlic in the pan. Cook until the chicken is no longer pink.
3. Bring the sugar, salt, and water to a boil. Turn down the heat and let it simmer for 30 minutes or until the chicken is cooked and soft.
4. Put in the scallions, celery, and boiled daikon. Cook for another 3 to 5 minutes.
5. Put the mixture into bowls for serving and top with celery leaves.

29. RICE AND BEEF SOUP

Prep Time: 30 Minutes | Cook Time: 1 Hour

Total Time: Minutes | Serving:

Ingredients

- 1 tbsp fresh parsley, chopped
- 1 tbsp fresh chives, chopped
- 1/2 tsp cinnamon, ground
- 1 1/2 cups of long grain rice
- 2 pounds beef, cubed
- salt and pepper
- 1 tbsp fresh rosemary, chopped
- 10 cups of water

Instructions

1. In a rice cooker that holds 10 cups of or more, put the rice, water, parsley, chives, rosemary, and pepper.
2. Just turn it on for a simple rice cooker. First, press the start button and set the rice cooker to the quick cook setting. Cover and let it heat up slowly.
3. Put the lid back on and cook for another hour. Then add the beef and cinnamon.

30. RICE COOKER BLACK BEANS

Prep Time: 5 Minutes | Cook Time: 2 Hour | Additional Time: 4 Hour 5 Minutes

Total Time: 6 Hour 10 Minutes | Serving: 4

Ingredients

- 1 cup of dried black beans
- 3 cups of water, or more as needed

Instructions

1. Cover the black beans with 3 cups of water. Wait five minutes. Throw away anything that floats to the top. Drain it.
2. Add three more cups of water on top of the black beans. Soak for four hours overnight. Drain it.
3. Put drained beans and 3 cups of water together in a rice cooker. Add more water if necessary and cook on the "Porridge" setting for about two hours or until soft. Drain it.

31. TACO SOUP IN THE RICE COOKER

Prep Time: 15 Minutes | Cook Time: 1 Hour

Total Time: 1 Hour 15 Minutes | Serving: 6

Ingredients

- 14 1/2 ounce diced tomatoes, canned
- 5 cup of chicken broth, low-sodium
- 1 cup of corn, canned
- 1 pound chicken breast
- 1/2 cup of black beans, canned
- 2 medium carrot
- 1 clove garlic
- 1 tbsp olive oil
- 1/2 cup of brown rice, raw
- 1/2 medium onion

Instructions

1. Cut up an onion and garlic and put them in the bottom of a HOT rice cooker with some oil. This will help them brown.
2. Cut your chicken while the onions and garlic heat in the rice cooker.
3. Put the chicken in the rice cooker until it turns brown.
4. Pour in chicken broth, tomato chunks, brown rice, and corn that has been drained. Rinse and drain the black beans. Peel and cut the carrots into small pieces.
5. Turn it on if your rice cooker has a "brown rice" setting. Otherwise, leave it on for at least an hour and a half.

32. BLACK PEPPER BEEF AND BROCCOLI FRIED RICE

Prep Time: 20 Minutes | Cook Time: 30 Minutes

Total Time: 50 Minutes | Serving: 4

Ingredients

- ♦ 2 tbsp of Oyster Sauce
- ♦ 3-4 cups of Rice cooked and cooled
- ♦ 1 tsp of Baking Soda
- ♦ 2 tbsp of Oil
- ♦ 3 tbsp of Corn Starch
- ♦ 2 cups of Broccoli
- ♦ 1.5pound of Beef
- ♦ 1.5tsp of Black Pepper

Sauce:

- ♦ 2.5 tbsp of Minced Garlic
- ♦ 0.5-1 tbsp of Black Pepper
- ♦ 2 tbsp of Oyster Sauce
- ♦ 2 tbsp of Ketchup
- ♦ 1 tbsp of Sugar
- ♦ 1.5 tbsp of Soy Sauce

Instructions

1. Follow these steps to cut the beef into thin slices. Then, mix 1.5 tsp of black pepper, two tbsp of oyster sauce, one tsp of baking soda, two tbsp of oil, and three tbsp of cornstarch. Let it sit for 10 to 20 minutes while you prepare the other things.
2. Mix peanut butter, black pepper, sugar, ketchup, oyster sauce, and soy sauce in a bowl.
3. Boil the broccoli for 30 seconds, then drain and set it aside.
4. Put some oil in a pan and raise the heat to medium-high. Put the beef in the hot pan and sit for 30 seconds. Then, saute it for two to three minutes.
5. After you add the broccoli, cook for one minute.
6. Mix the rice with the sauce and cook it on high heat for two to three minutes.

33. PINEAPPLE PORK FRIED RICE

Prep Time: 30 Minutes | Cook Time: 15 Minutes

Total Time: 45 Minutes | Serving: 4

Ingredients

- 3 tbsp reduced-sodium soy sauce
- 2 tsp grated fresh ginger
- 1 pound pork tenderloin, cut into bite-size pieces
- ½ cup of thinly sliced carrot (1 medium)
- 2 cups of cooked jasmine rice
- ½ cup of sliced scallions
- 2 tsp canola oil plus 1 tbsp, divided
- ½ cup of frozen peas, thawed
- ½ cup of thinly bias-sliced celery (1 stalk)
- 2 egg whites
- 2 cloves garlic, minced
- 1 cup of chopped fresh pineapple
- 1 egg
- 1 tbsp snipped fresh cilantro

Instructions

1. In a small bowl, beat the egg and egg whites together. Set this bowl aside. Put two tsp of oil in a considerable skillet heat it over medium-high heat. Put in pork. Stir-fry it for three to five minutes or until the pork is no longer pink. Take the pork out of the pan and set it aside.

2. Put the 1 tbsp of oil to the pan or wok. Stir-fry the vegetables for three to four minutes or until they are soft. Add the pineapple, carrot, celery, scallions, and ginger. Stir-fry for 30 seconds more after adding the garlic. Put in the egg mix and wait 5 to 10 seconds until the egg sets on the bottom but stays runny on top. Put in cooked rice. Toss and turn the mixture all the time for one minute. Add the cooked pork, peas, soy sauce, and cilantro, and heat everything. Serve right away.

34. VEGETABLE RICE PILAF IN THE RICE COOKER

Prep Time: 20 Minutes | Cook Time: 50 Minutes

Total Time: 1 Hour 10 Minutes | Serving: 6

Ingredients

- 3 ½ cups of water
- 1 carrot, chopped
- 1 tsp chicken bouillon granules
- 3 tsp chicken bouillon granules
- 3 green onions, chopped
- 4 mushrooms, chopped
- ¼ cup of water, or more if needed
- 4 small heads baby bok choy, trimmed and chopped
- 3 cups of uncooked white rice
- ground black pepper to taste

Instructions

1. Mix three tsp of chicken bouillon in a rice cooker with 3 1/2 cups of water.
2. The bouillon and water should be mixed with rice, baby bok choy, green onions, carrots, and mushrooms.
3. Start the rice cooker and cook it for about 50 minutes, or until the rice is soft and the liquid is absorbed.
4. Mix one-fourth cup of water and 1 tsp of chicken bouillon in a small bowl. Then, put the mixture into a blender.
5. Put a cup of rice and bouillon mixture into a blender. Blend until the mixture turns into a thin paste, adding more water if needed.
6. Combine the rice paste with the rest of the cooked vegetables and rice, and mix it all well. Add black pepper.

35. PORK FRIED RICE

Prep Time: 15 Minutes | Cook Time: 20 Minutes

Total Time: 35 Minutes | Serving: 6

Ingredients

- 1 tbsp unsalted butter
- 1 tbsp sesame oil
- 1 bunch green onions thinly sliced, divided
- 2 tbsp canola oil or grapeseed or avocado oil divided
- 1 tsp kosher salt plus additional to taste
- 1/2 tsp ground black pepper plus additional to taste
- 1 small pork tenderloin (about 1 pound) trimmed and cut into 3/4-inch cubes

- 3 tbsp oyster sauce
- 3 large eggs
- 1 tbsp minced garlic about 3 cloves garlic
- 2 red bell peppers diced
- 3 cups of leftover COLD cooked brown rice
- 3 tbsp reduced sodium soy sauce
- 1 (10- to 12-ounce) bag frozen peas and carrots thawed
- 1 tbsp minced fresh ginger

Instructions

1. Salt and pepper the pork cubes and toss them. Mix the soy, oyster, and sesame oil in a small bowl.
2. Heat the oil over high heat in a big wok or strong skillet. Add the pork when the oil gets hot and starts to shimmer. It will take about 5 minutes to cook until fully cooked and brown on all sides. Put the food in a big bowl.
3. Put in half a tbsp of oil. Place the frozen vegetables and bell pepper in the bowl. For about 5 to 10 minutes, stir the pepper now and then until it softens and turns brown. Move to the bowl with the pork using a slotted spoon.
4. Take the pan off the heat. Add the last 1/2 tbsp of oil. Add the garlic and ginger and mix them. Cook for about 15 seconds or until the food smells good.
5. Bring the pan back to medium to high heat and add the rice, half of the green onions, and butter. Break up any clumps as you stir, and then add the butter and oil and coat it all.
6. Form a well in the middle of the rice, move it to one side, and crack the eggs into the space. Scramble with a fork, then leave to cook for a while. Break the eggs up and add them to the rice when they are almost done cooking.
7. Add the rest of the green onions, the vegetables you set aside, the pork (along with any juices that have been collected), and the sauce to the skillet. Mix everything and cover it all with the sauce. Try it and change the seasonings as needed. Have it hot.

36. RICE COOKER MUSHROOM RISOTTO

Prep Time: 5 Minutes | Cook Time: 30 Minutes

Total Time: 35 Minutes | Serving: 6

Ingredients

- 1/2 cup of finely chopped onion
- 1/2 tsp salt
- 1 1/2 cups of Arborio rice, rinsed and drained well
- 2 tbsp chopped fresh parsley
- 8 ounces mushrooms, cleaned and sliced
- 1/4 tsp pepper
- 1 clove garlic, minced
- 2 tbsp butter
- 3 to 3 1/2 cups of low-sodium chicken or vegetable broth
- 2 tbsp olive oil
- 1/2 cup of grated Parmesan cheese, plus more for serving

Instructions

1. In the rice cooker's bowl, put the rice that has been rinsed and drained. Put one tbsp of the olive oil on top and stir to coat well. Put in the salt and 2 1/2 cups of broth. Mix well.
2. Lock the lid and press the "Cook" button to cook the rice. Put it on "Keep Warm" for 20 minutes and then finish cooking.
3. Make the rice. Heat the one tbsp of olive oil in a large, heavy skillet over medium-low heat. Add the onion and stir it around a lot while cooking for about 5 minutes or until it's soft.
4. After adding the garlic, stir it and cook for another minute or two.
5. Put the pepper and mushrooms in there. For 5 to 8 minutes, stirring often, cook until the mushrooms are juicy and soft. The pan should no longer be hot. If you think it needs it, add more salt and pepper to taste. Put away.
6. Put the rice cooker on "Keep Warm." Then, carefully open the lid and add the sauteed mushrooms and an extra 1/2 cup of broth, butter, parsley, and Parmesan cheese. The mixture should be smooth and creamy. If not, add up to another 1/2 cup of broth and mix it in.
7. Stir for another minute or so, then taste it and make any more changes to the seasonings you think are needed. If you want, you can serve it with extra Parmesan cheese on top.

37. SWEET AND SOUR PORK

Prep Time: 15 Minutes | Cook Time: 3 Hour

Total Time: 3 Hour 15 Minutes | Serving: 8

Ingredients

- sliced green onions for garnish
- 1 green bell pepper
- 2 pounds boneless pork loin chops
- 2 tbsp ketchup
- 2 tbsp tapioca flour or cornstarch whisked with equal amount of water
- 1/4 cup of brown sugar
- 2 tbsp rice vinegar
- 20 ounce can pineapple chunks drained and juice reserved
- 1 yellow or white onion
- 1 red bell pepper
- 2 tbsp soy sauce
- 1/4 cup of reserved pineapple juice from can

Instructions

1. Get pork and put it in the slow cooker. Cut it up into chewy pieces.
2. Cut onions into 1-inch pieces after peeling them.
3. Take pepper stems and seeds off and cut them into 1-inch pieces.
4. Toss the chicken in the slow cooker with the onions, peppers, and pineapple.
5. In a bowl, whisk together everything else except the green onions.
6. Pour over the things in the slow cooker.
7. Put the lid on top and cook on high for three to four hours or low for six to eight hours.
8. Serve with rice and green onions on top, or however you like.

38. STEWED PORK CABBAGE RICE

Prep Time: 10 Minutes | Cook Time: 20 Minutes

Total Time: 30 Minutes | Serving: 4

Ingredients

- 1/3 cup of water or low sodium chicken stock
- 2 cans of stewed pork chops bones and fats removed, gravy reserved 3-4 shiitake mushrooms stems removed and diced
- 1/2 cabbage chopped into small pieces (about 1-1/2 cups)
- 2 cups of rice rinsed
- 1/4 tsp sugar
- 4-5 slices of old ginger 1 tbsp dark soy
- 2-3 cloves garlic smashed
- 1 tbsp butter optional
- White pepper to taste
- 1 tbsp light soy or to taste
- Coriander and sliced red chilli to garnish

Instructions

1. Cut up the pork into smaller pieces.
2. Put the rice in the cooker, and then add the two cans of gravy you saved.
3. One tbsp each of dark soy, light soy, sugar, and white pepper. Mix the rice around. Pork stew, mushrooms, garlic, ginger, and cabbage should all be added.
4. Mix it up and cook it usually.
5. After the rice is done, let it sit for 5 minutes. Then, add butter and fluff up the rice while you mix in the softened garlic. To taste, add more soy if you need to.
6. Take out the ginger slices before serving. Add the coriander and chili slices as a garnish, and then serve.

39. RICE COOKER GREEN RICE

Prep Time: 10 Minutes | Cook Time: 20 Minutes

Total Time: 30 Minutes | Serving: 4

Ingredients

- 2 poblano chiles
- 1 medium yellow onion, finely diced
- 1 tsp kosher salt
- 4 scallions, sliced (optional)
- black pepper
- 2 cups of chicken stock
- 1 cup of cilantro
- 1 cup of white rice
- 1 tbsp vegetable oil
- 3 garlic cloves

Instructions

1. Make big pieces out of the chiles. To make rice less spicy, take out the seeds and veins. To make rice much more spicy, leave them in. Sometimes, I take out the seeds but leave the veins.
2. Put the garlic cloves, cilantro leaves, salt, and pepper pieces into a blender. Add 1/2 cup of chicken stock. Mix until it's smooth. If you need to, add more chicken stock to make blending easier.
3. In the meantime, put oil in a small skillet and heat it over medium heat. Cook the onion until it gets soft. Stir for one more minute after adding the rice.
4. Add the rice and onion mix into the rice cooker. Put the rest of the chicken stock and the chile puree. Set the rice cooker to "cook" and give it a quick stir.
5. When the cooking time is up, fluff the rice. There may be crusty rice on the bottom of the pot; this is the best rice. The rice may need a few more minutes of steaming on the warm setting before it reaches your desired consistency.
6. You can add lime juice, salt, and pepper to taste. You can put green onion slices on top.

40. BEEF AND RICE CASSEROLE

Prep Time: 10 Minutes | Cook Time: 30 Minutes

Total Time: 40 Minutes | Serving: 12

Ingredients

- 1 tbsp Worcestershire sauce
- 1 medium red bell pepper, diced
- 3 cloves garlic, minced
- 1 ½ cups of beef broth or stock
- 1 medium yellow onion, diced
- 10 ounce can Rotel Diced Tomatoes & Green Chilies - Do not drain
- 1 pound lean ground beef
- 1 cup of long grain rice
- 1 ½ cups of shredded Cheddar cheese
- Chopped fresh parsley for garnish if desired
- 1 tsp salt
- 1 tsp pepper

Instructions

1. In a big pan over medium-low heat, brown the ground beef with the salt, garlic, and pepper. Put the food back on the stove over medium heat after draining.
2. Add the onion, peppers, and garlic and mix them in. The onions and peppers will get softer after another 3 to 4 minutes of cooking.
3. Add the rice, Rotel that has yet to be drained, Worcestershire sauce, and beef broth to the pan. Stir the ingredients together until they are well mixed.
4. Bring everything to a boil, then turn down the heat and cover. Keep cooking for 20 minutes more or until the rice is soft.
5. Take it off the heat and add a lot of cheese on top. Put the lid on the pan and let the food sit for 5 minutes. This will help the cheese melt and get all gooey.
6. For extra flavor, you can add chopped parsley as a garnish.

41. PORK AND BROWN RICE GREEN CHILE CASSEROLE

Prep Time: 5 Minutes | Cook Time: 25 Minutes

Total Time: 30 Minutes | Serving: 8

Ingredients

- 2 tbsp fresh minced garlic (or to taste)
- 1/4 cup of chicken broth or 1/4 cup of water
- 1 1/2 tbsp cumin (can use more)
- 1/2 cup of salsa
- 2 (4 ounce) cans green chili peppers
- 1 1/2 cups of instant brown rice, uncooked
- 1 small jalapeno pepper, seeded and finely chopped (optional or to taste)
- 2 cups of shredded cheddar cheese, divided
- 4 tbsp oil (more if needed)
- salt and black pepper
- 2 onions, chopped
- 1 (10 ounce) can cream of chicken soup, undiluted
- 1 1/2 pounds boneless pork loin chops (cut into small bite-size pieces)
- 1 (14 ounce) can Rotel Tomatoes (or use diced tomatoes)
- 1 (15 ounce) can black beans, rinsed and drained

Instructions

1. In a big, heavy saucepan, heat the oil over medium-low heat.
2. Then, add the pork to the hot oil and cook on all sides until it becomes light brown. Take it out and put it in a bowl.
3. Put the garlic and onion in the pan and cook for three to four minutes.
4. Put the meat back in the pot and then add the rice, cream of chicken soup, Jalapeno pepper, black beans, green chilies, salsa, water or broth, and cumin. Mix everything well, then cover the pot and cook on medium heat for 20-25 minutes.
5. Please put it in a casserole dish and sprinkle about 1 1/2 cups of cheddar cheese.
6. Heat the dish in the oven to 350 degrees and melt the cheese.

42. RICE COOKER CHILI

Prep Time: 5 Minutes | Cook Time: 35 Minutes

Total Time: 40 Minutes | Serving: 3

Ingredients

- 1/2 pound. ground beef
- 1/2 6ounce. can tomato paste
- 1/2 tsp salt
- 1 15ounce. can kidney beans
- 1/2 tsp cumin
- 1/8 tsp cayenne pepper
- 1 15ounce. can diced tomatoes

- 1 Tbsp olive oil
- 1/2 Tbsp chili powder
- 3/4 cup of water
- 1/4 tsp garlic powder
- 1 tsp brown sugar
- freshly cracked pepper
- 1/2 tsp onion powder

Instructions

1. Put the ground beef and olive oil in the rice cooker. Choose the "white rice" or "cook" function, depending on what your cooker can do. Close the lid and cook the beef. Open it for a moment every couple of minutes to stir and break up the meat. Do this for about 5 minutes or until the beef is fully browned. Many rice cookers, like the one I used, will heat up once the lid is shut, so remember to do that every time you stir the rice.

2. If the beef you are using has a lot of fat, drain the extra fat after it has browned all the way through. In a rice cooker, add the ground beef and mix in the cayenne, chili powder, garlic powder, cumin, onion powder, brown sugar, salt, and pepper. Then, cover the rice cooker and cook for one minute more.

3. Add the kidney beans, tomato paste, water, and diced tomatoes (with their juices) to the rice cooker. Make sure the kidney beans are drained. Mix everything by stirring it.

4. Once more, close the lid and make sure "cook" or "white rice" is chosen. Then, let the chili simmer for 30 minutes. Ensure the chili doesn't stick to the bottom by stirring it occasionally. Start the cycle over if the 30 minutes are up and your cooker is still cooking.

5. After 30 minutes of simmering, taste the chili and add more seasoning if you like. Then, serve with your favorite chili toppings.

43. RICE COOKER RICE PILAF

Prep Time: 5 Minutes | Cook Time: 30 Minutes

Total Time: 35 Minutes | Serving: 4

Ingredients

- ¼ cup of onion, chopped
- ¼ cup of slivered almonds
- 1 tbsp butter
- 1 clove garlic, minced
- 1 bay leaf
- 1 ¼ cup of chicken broth
- ½ tsp kosher salt
- 1 cup of mushrooms, diced
- 1 cup of Jasmine Rice use US measuring (dry)

Instructions

1. Make sure to wash and rinse the rice well.
2. The chicken broth, onion, garlic, butter, bay leaf, almonds, rice, and kosher salt should all be added to the rice cooker pot. Add the things and mix them well.
3. Use the white rice setting on the cooker to start cooking.
4. Use a small plastic spoon to fluff the rice when it's done, and serve!

44. PILAU RICE

Prep Time: 5 Minutes | Cook Time: 30 Minutes

Total Time: 35 Minutes | Serving: 1

Ingredients

- 1 small onion finely chopped
- 1 cup of basmati rice (rice cooker cup)
- 1 green cardamom pod crushed
- Pinch sea salt
- 2 whole cloves
- 1 tsp turmeric
- 2 tsp vegetable oil
- 1/4 tsp cumin powder
- 1 tej patta bay leaf
- 1/4 cinnamon stick

Instructions

1. The basmati rice should be washed three or four times in cold water until the water is clear. Remove all the water and set it aside. Put the sea salt, whole cloves, crushed cardamom, bay leaf, and cinnamon stick in a tiny bowl. Set it aside.
2. Place the pan on medium warm and add the oil. Stir-fry the onion until it gets soft, which should take about 3 minutes. Put in the bowl of spices you just made, and stir-fry for one minute. When you add the washed and drained rice, ensure it's well mixed with the oil and spices.
3. Add enough water to reach the first mark on the pot to cover the ingredients from the frying pan. Fill up the inner pot of your rice cooker. Use the "white/long grain" setting to cook the rice. When the rice is done, use a rice spoon to mix it well. Then, remove the spices and set the stove to "keep warm" for 10 minutes. Once more, combine the rice well to make it fluffy, and then serve it with your favorite curry dishes.

45. EDAMAME RICE

Prep Time: 15 Minutes | Cook Time: 30 Minutes

Total Time: 45 Minutes | Serving: 4

Ingredients

- ♦ 2 rice cups of (2 rice cups of equals 1 ½ regular cups of)
- ♦ ¼ cup of nametake
- ♦ ¼ cup of shelled edamame, cooked
- ♦ ¼ cup of ochazuke wakame

Instructions

1. Get the rice ready. The rice should be washed several times or until the water is almost clear.
2. Make the rice. (Use the same amount of water and cooking setting you usually use for rice in the rice cooker.)
3. Add the ochazuke wakame to the rice when it's done cooking. Mix slowly with a rice paddle. Add the name. Mix it again.
4. Put in the cooked edamame. Once more, mix until everything is well mixed.
5. All set to eat!

46. 10 MINUTE RAINBOW FRIED RICE

Prep Time: 10 Minutes | Cook Time: 10 Minutes

Total Time: 20 Minutes | Serving: 4

Ingredients

- 2 tbsps Sweet Corn
- 2 tbsps Cauliflower
- 2 tbsps Carrots
- 2 tbsps Broccoli
- 2 cups of water (or as indicated on the rice cooker)
- 2 cups of Rice (I'm using brown rice)
- 2 tbsps Cherry Tomatoes
- 2 Eggs
- 1 tbsp onions or shallots, minced
- 2 tbsps Protein of Choice (optional)

Seasoning Sauce:

- 2 tbsps Oyster Sauce
- 2 tbsps Dark Soy Sauce
- 1 tsp Salt
- 2 tbsps Light Soy Sauce
- 1 tsp Garlic, minced
- 1 tsp Black Pepper
- 2 tbsps Sambal Oelek or Sriracha (optional)

Instructions

1. Make sure the water runs clear when you wash the rice. Put them in the rice cooker pot and add enough water to cover them. Then follow the directions on the rice cooker pot. In general, rice and water should be mixed 1:1.
2. Next, add the onions and mix them into the rice.
3. You can put any rainbow vegetable, like corn, broccoli, cherry tomatoes, tomatoes, or cauliflower, in the center of the rice in the rice cooker pot. Add eggs on top.
4. Put the lid back on the rice cooker and set it to the normal rice settings!
5. Make the seasoning sauce at the same time. Simply put all the ingredients in a bowl and mix them.
6. Rainbow rice is done when the counter beeps. Open the lid right away, add the sauce, and use the rice paddle to mix everything while it's still hot. Done!

47. HERB LEMON RICE RECIPE

Prep Time: 5 Minutes | Cook Time: 20 Minutes

Total Time: 25 Minutes | Serving: 4

Ingredients

- 1 tbsp coconut oil
- 1 tsp dried oregano
- 1 cup of basmati rice rinsed
- ¼ tsp salt
- 1 tsp dried basil
- 2 cups of stock
- ½ lemon zested

After Cooking:

- ½ lemon juiced

Instructions

1. Basmati rice, coconut oil, salt, lemon zest, dried basil, oregano, and stock should all be put into a rice cooker together. Use the "white rice" function to cook.
2. After cooking, add the lemon juice and serve.

48. RICE COOKER NO SOAK LOR MA GAI

Prep Time: 15 Minutes | Cook Time: 50 Minutes

Total Time: 1 hour 5 Minutes | Serving: 2

Ingredients

- 1 cup of glutinous rice, rinsed until water runs clear
- 1 cup of water or stock

To Pan Fry:

- 1 garlic, minced
- 1 cm ginger, grated
- 1 tbsp dried shrimps, soaked in warm water for 10 mins
- 2 shiitake mushrooms, sliced
- 1 tbsp cooking oil
- 1 tsp sesame oil
- 70g char siu chicken
- 60g minced meat
- 1-2 stalks of chives (or sprint onions), chopped
- 1 shallot, minced
- 8 pepperoni slices (optional)

Seasoning Sauce:

- 1 tbsp light soy sauce
- 1/2 tsp white pepper
- 1 tbsp oyster sauce
- 2 tbsps dark soy sauce

Instructions

Rice Cooker:

1. A pan should have oil in it. Add the shallot, ginger, and garlic when the oil is hot. Once the food smells good, add the ground meat and dried shrimp. To almost cook the ground meat, stir-fry it.
2. Put the mushrooms and the seasoning sauce in the pan. Stir everything up. Let the mushrooms soak up the sauce before adding the pepperoni and char siu. Put in the sesame oil and mix it in. Turn off the heat.
3. Rinse the glutinous rice, then add it to the rice cooker pot. Put the pan-fried foods and all of the sauces into the rice cooker pot. Put in stock or water. Fold the rice in half and pat it down to make it flat.
4. Set the rice cooker to "sweet rice," or set the timer for 50 minutes and turn it on. After half an hour, you can stir the rice all the way through to make it even, but it's unnecessary.
5. Add the chives to the cooked rice, and lo ma gai is ready to be served! Put the rice in a bowl and then turn it onto a plate to make it look nice.

Rice Cooker with One Setting:

1. Wash glutinous rice and let it soak for two hours. Drain after soaking.
2. To make rice, do steps 1 through 3 again.
3. Press "Start" and wait for the rice to cook. When the cooking time is up, the sticky rice should be fully cooked. Add the chives as a garnish and serve.

Steaming:

1. Cleanse the glutinous rice and let it soak for at least 4 hours. Drain after soaking.
2. Do steps 1 and 2 again in "Rice Cooker." Add the drained glutinous rice after you've stirred in the sesame oil. Add the rice and stir it in with the things in the pan. Fill bowls that can hold steam with glutinous rice after mixing it evenly.
3. Start the steamer and put the bowls of glutinous rice inside it. Let it steam for about 40 minutes or until the rice is done. Add the chives as a garnish and serve.

49. CHEESY BROCCOLI RICE

Prep Time: 5 Minutes | Cook Time: 25 Minutes

Total Time: 30 Minutes | Serving: 6

Ingredients

- ¾ cup of grated cheddar cheese
- 4 cups of chicken broth
- 3 cups of fresh or frozen broccoli florets
- 1 tsp table salt
- Salt and pepper to taste
- 1-1/2 cups of arborio rice
- 2 tbsp dried minced onions
- 1 tbsp minced garlic
- 2 Tbsp butter

Instructions

1. Mix the rice, butter, minced onions, garlic, broth, salt, and black pepper in the rice cooker. Mix everything.
2. Close the lid on the rice cooker and press the down button on the cook switch. It will take about 25 minutes for the rice to cook.
3. Put broccoli and half as much water as it will hold in a small saucepan while the rice is cooking. Over medium-low heat, bring to a boil. Strain and set aside.
4. Add the broccoli and cheese when the rice cooker turns to WARM.

50. SALMON RICE

Prep Time: 5 Minutes | Cook Time: 20 Minutes

Total Time: 25 Minutes | Serving: 3-4

Ingredients

- 1 tbsp sake
- 2 6-8 ounce boneless salmon fillets
- 2 scallions, finely chopped
- 1 thumb size ginger, peeled and sliced into thin strips
- 1 ½ tsp dashi powder
- 1 ½ tbsp soy sauce
- 2 cups of Japanese short grain rice

Instructions

1. Take the rice out of the water and rinse it well. Then put it in the inner pot of the rice cooker.
2. Fill the cup with water until it reads 2 cups, then add the sake, soy sauce, and dashi. Use a stir to mix. On top of the rice, put the salmon fillets and ginger. Then, close the lid.
3. In the menu, choose "Plain" and press "Start."
4. Break up the salmon with the rice paddle and mix it into the rice when it's done cooking. Now, you can take off the skin.
5. Place the rice in a bowl for serving and sprinkle scallions on top. Serve it.

51. RICE COOKER LAP CHEONG RICE

Prep Time: 5 Minutes | Cook Time: 20 Minutes

Total Time: 25 Minutes | Serving: 3

Ingredients

- water
- 2 cup of jasmine rice
- lap cheong (Chinese Sausage)

Instructions

1. Determine how much rice you want by measuring it in your rice cooker cup (2 cups is ideal for three people).
2. Next, add water to the rice cooker until it reaches the line where the number of cups is indicated. As an alternative, you can use the "finger trick," which involves measuring the height of the rice (even it out first) along your finger and then adding water to your finger, if you rest it on top of the rice, to equal that height.
3. The rice cooker should be turned on after adding the Chinese sausage (one link per person is a good bet). Steaming the rice and sausage simultaneously is what the cooker does! Once the sausage is sliced, serve it with the rice.

52. TURMERIC (YELLOW) BASMATI RICE

Prep Time: 5 Minutes | Cook Time: 30 Minutes

Total Time: 35 Minutes | Serving: 4

Ingredients

- 1 tsp minced garlic
- 1 tbsp melted butter
- ¼ cup of minced yellow onion
- 1 bay leaf
- ½ tsp turmeric powder
- 1 cup of basmati rice use US measuring (dry) cup
- 1 ½ cups of chicken broth
- ¼ tsp kosher salt

Instructions

1. In the microwave, melt the butter for 15 to 20 seconds.
2. Using a mesh strainer to rinse the rice. Make sure you thoroughly shake off any extra water.
3. In the pot, combine the rice, butter, onion, garlic, turmeric, bay leaf, and salt. Stir thoroughly.
4. Mix the ingredients together and put the chicken stock.
5. Depending on how the rice cooker works, set it to cook or to start.
6. When finished, use a fork to fluff and serve.

53. RICE COOKER THAI STRAWBERRY STICKY RICE

Prep Time: 10 Minutes | Cook Time: 30 Minutes

Total Time: 40 Minutes | Serving: 3-4

Ingredients

- ¼ Condensed milk
- 1 cup of Coconut milk
- Pinch salt
- 2 cups of Sweet rice (also called Thai sticky rice)
- 6-8 Fresh strawberries, chopped
- 2 ½ cup of Water
- Mint leaves, optional

Instructions

1. Set the rice cooker's inner pot with the sweet rice, water, and salt inside and leave it for half an hour. Once the [Plain] function is selected, click "Start."
2. A bowl should be used to combine the condensed milk and coconut milk in the meantime. Set it aside.
3. After cooking, separate the rice into four to six dishes. Top the rice with ¼ cup of coconut milk sauce, strawberries, and mint leaves. Put to use.

54. CORN RICE

Prep Time: 10 Minutes | Cook Time: 20 Minutes

Total Time: 30 Minutes | Serving: 3-4

Ingredients

- 1 tsp salt
- 2 cups of short grain Japanese rice (use the supplied measuring cup)
- 2 tbsp cooking sake
- Ground black pepper
- 1 small can corn (8.75 ounces), rinsed and drained
- 2 tbsp butter

Instructions

1. After giving the rice a thorough rinse in cold water, continue tossing it until the water turns clear.
2. After transferring the rice to the inner pot of the rice cooker, fill it with water to the 2-cup of mark for white rice. Stir in the corn, sake, and salt.
3. Shut the lid, select the [Plain] option, and hit the start button. Once the cover is open, add the butter.
4. Add a small pinch of ground black pepper, toss well to coat the rice evenly, and then serve.

55. RIBS AND RICE

Prep Time: 1 Hour | Cook Time: 35 Minutes

Total Time: 1 hour 35 Minutes | Serving: 4

Ingredients

To Marinate The Ribs:

- 1/3 tsp salt
- 1/4 tsp dark soy sauce
- 1 pound pork ribs
- 1/4 tsp white pepper

You'll Also Need:

- 3 slices ginger (chopped)
- 3-5 cloves garlic (chopped)
- 1/2 cup of carrots (diced)
- Water
- 1/2 cup of water
- 1 tsp salt
- 8 dried shiitake mushrooms
- 1/2 tsp sugar
- 2 tbsp oil
- 1/4 cup of peas (fresh or frozen)
- 2 cups of uncooked rice
- 2 tsp light soy sauce

Instructions

1. After tossing the ribs with the marinade, let them sit for an hour.
2. One tbsp of oil should be heated over medium heat in a wok when you're ready to cook. When the mushrooms are caramelized, add them and stir-fry. Take out of the wok and place aside.
3. Brown the marinated ribs in the wok with an additional tbsp of oil, this time over high heat. After browning, reduce the flame to medium and mix in the sugar, ginger, and garlic. After a minute of stir-frying, incorporate the carrots, ½ cup of water, and light soy sauce. After bringing it to a simmer, cook for five to ten minutes or until nearly all of the liquid evaporates.
4. Put the rice in the rice cooker and the appropriate amount of water (based on the type of rice you're using and the directions provided) while the ribs are simmering. At this point, if preferred, you can drain the mushrooms and add some of the liquid they were soaking in. As an alternative, you might use vegetable, pig, or chicken stock.
5. Add one tsp of salt and the shiitake mushrooms and stir. To ensure that the rice and liquid are evenly distributed, give the pot a gentle shake. Cover the rice with the rib mixture. Press the button to initiate the rice cooker after placing it inside. We're about to start your supper.
6. The majority of rice cookers available nowadays will indicate the remaining cooking time in minutes. After 5 minutes of cooking, open the rice cooker lid, quickly add the peas, cover the lid right away, and allow the rice cooker to finish cooking. Once it's finished, serve!

56. FIVE SPICE CHICKEN IN RICE COOKER

Prep Time: 15 Minutes | Cook Time: 35 Minutes

Total Time: 50 Minutes | Serving: 4

Ingredients

- 10 shallots, peeled and roughly chopped
- 4 scallions, cut into 2 inch pieces
- 3 tbsp Shaoxing wine
- 4 chicken legs

Marinating sauce:

- 1 tbsp five spice powder
- 2 inch ginger, grated
- 1 tsp salt
- 1 tbsp sesame oil
- 1 tsp ground white pepper

Instructions

1. Apply the marinating sauce to the chicken legs in a mixing bowl. Place a saran plastic wrap over the bowl and refrigerate for approximately half an hour.
2. In a rice cooker pot, place the shallots and scallions at the bottom. Arrange the chicken over the shallots and onions and pour Shaoxing wine over it.
3. After 30 minutes of cooking in the rice cooker, turn it to "warm" and wait an additional five minutes.
4. Carefully remove the rice cooker cover to reveal a piping-hot layer of steam, and use a small knife or skewer to test if the chicken is done. The chicken is done if the liquid runs clear. If not, simmer for a further five minutes or until the juice flows clear.
5. Spoon onto a serving platter and serve hot over steaming white rice right away.

57. RICE COOKER THAI MASAMAN CURRY

Prep Time: 20 Minutes | Cook Time: 2 Hour 30 Minutes

Total Time: 2 Hour 50 Minutes | Serving: 4-5

Ingredients

- ♦ 3 cups of cubed butter squash
- ♦ 2 cups of sliced carrots
- ♦ 2 tbsp Masaman curry paste
- ♦ 2 tbsp fish sauce
- ♦ 2 chicken breast
- ♦ 1 cup of chopped yellow onion
- ♦ ½ cup of edamame beans
- ♦ 1 tbsp Stevia brown sugar
- ♦ ½ cup of uncook brown jasmine rice
- ♦ 4 ½ cups of low-sodium chicken stock
- ♦ ½ cup of lite coconut milk
- ♦ ¼ cup of diced fresh ginger

Instructions

1. Assemble every component by chopping, slicing, cutting, and dicing.
2. Next, arrange all of them in a rice cooker pot. Start with an item that will take longer to cook, such as butter squash or chicken breast, and pile the remaining ingredients on top.
3. If your rice cooker has a brown rice button, select it and pour in the chicken stock and light coconut milk before cooking.
4. Give it two hours and thirty minutes to cook. Take a bowlful and savor it.

58. CHINESE PUMPKIN RICE

Prep Time: 10 Minutes | Cook Time: 25 Minutes

Total Time: 35 Minutes | Serving: 4

Ingredients

- 1½ Cups of pumpkin
- 1½-2 Tbsp light soy sauce
- ¼ tsp white pepper
- 1 Tbsp oyster sauce
- 2 Tbsp dried shrimp
- 5 cloves garlic
- 1 Tbsp dark soy sauce
- 1 tsp white sugar

Instructions

1. To boil the rice, drain the dried shrimp and reserve the soaking water.
2. To make the dried shrimp crispy, pan-fry them in a small amount of oil. If you have extra, spread it out on paper towels to absorb excess oil so you can use it as a garnish for rice later.
3. In the same pan as the remaining shrimp, add the minced garlic and stir-fry over low heat until fragrant. Garlic is prone to burning.
4. Include the rinsed rice. The oil will spark, so proceed with caution. Increase the heat to medium-high and stir-fry the grains for a brief toasting.
5. Place everything into the pot of the rice cooker. Once the prawns have soaked, add extra (normal) water until your index finger reaches the first line.
6. Add the sauces to the pot after adding the pumpkin cubes. To begin cooking, add the pepper and white sugar and hit the button!
7. After the rice cooker finishes cooking, let it undisturbed for an additional five minutes, then uncover, fluff it up gently, and serve.

59. EASY RICE COOKER FRIED RICE WITH EGG

Prep Time: 10 Minutes | Cook Time: 40 Minutes

Total Time: 50 Minutes | Serving: 4

Ingredients

- ¼ tsp sugar
- ½ tbsp butter
- 1 egg, lightly whisked
- ¾ cups of Chinese sausage, cut into ½" thick rounds, then halved 2 links
- ¾ cup of frozen vegetables
- green onions garnish
- 1 cup of Jasmine rice use US measuring (dry) cup
- 1 tsp fish sauce
- 1 ¼ cup of chicken broth
- ¼ cup of onion, chopped
- 2 cloves garlic, minced
- 1 tsp soy sauce

Instructions

1. Using a mesh strainer to rinse the rice. Make sure you thoroughly shake off any extra water.
2. Rice, broth, butter, fish sauce, soy sauce, garlic, and onion should all be added. After that, spin it to combine.
3. Over the water, scatter the vegetables, sausage, and beaten egg.
4. Depending on how the rice cooker works, set it to cook or to start.
5. When cooked, use a fork to fluff, then top with green onions before serving.

60. RED BEANS AND RICE

Prep Time: 5 Minutes | Cook Time: 15 Minutes

Total Time: 20 Minutes | Serving: 4

Ingredients

- ♦ 3-4 garlic cloves minced
- ♦ 2 ½ cups of water
- ♦ 10 ounces RoTel
- ♦ 1 cup of long grain white rice
- ♦ 2 Tbsp tomato paste
- ♦ 16 ounces kidney beans rinsed and drained

Instructions

1. After adding all of the ingredients, select WHITE RICE on the rice cooker.
2. Once done, stir and savor.

61. RICE COOKER TERIYAKI SHRIMP AND RICE

Prep Time: 10 Minutes | Cook Time: 30 Minutes

Total Time: 40 Minutes | Serving: 4

Ingredients

- 2 cloves garlic, minced
- 1/4 cup of soy sauce
- 1.5 cups of uncooked jasmine rice
- 2 Tbsp brown sugar
- 1/2 pound raw medium shrimp
- 1 tsp grated fresh ginger
- 1 cup of frozen peas
- 1 small onion
- 2 cups of water

Instructions

1. If the shrimp is frozen, pour cool water over it in a colander to thaw it first; this should take a few minutes.
2. Chop the onion finely and put it in the rice cooker's bottom, along with the frozen peas. Add the grated ginger, minced garlic, and uncooked rice. Mix these components together.
3. After adding the shrimp to the rice mixture, add two cups of water. Once the cooker is on the "white rice" setting, close the lid. When the rice cooker's internal temperature reaches the proper level, it will start to count down the cooking time.
4. Before opening the cover, let the rice cooker sit on the keep warm mode for a further five to ten minutes after the cooking cycle is complete. Stir the brown sugar and soy sauce together while you wait.
5. Lastly, remove the lid and cover the rice cooker's contents with the soy sauce mixture. Gently incorporate the sauce into the rice using a rice paddle. If preferred, top hot dishes with chopped green onions or Sriracha.

62. SCALLOPS AND RICE

Prep Time: 20 Minutes | Cook Time: 1 Hour

Total Time: 1 Hour 20 Minutes | Serving: 2

Ingredients

- ♦ ½ pound fresh scallops
- ♦ 1 tbsp sake
- ♦ 1 tbsp soy sauce
- ♦ 2 tbsp butter
- ♦ 2 cups of rice
- ♦ 2 tbsp chopped green onions or chives
- ♦ 1.5 cups of water

Instructions

1. Get the scallops ready. Salt the scallops on both sides just a little bit. Transfer to a plate and refrigerate for fifteen minutes (do not cover the plate).
2. Get the rice ready. Repeatedly wash the rice (until the water is nearly clear). Add the rice, sake, and soy sauce to the rice pot along with the water. Give it a fifteen-minute rest.
3. Take the scallops out of the refrigerator. After patting dry, arrange the scallops over the rice, with the water covering them. Keep still.
4. Use the same basic rice cooker setting that you would normally use to cook rice while making scallop rice. After cooking, give it a five-minute rest.
5. Take out the rice cooker's rice pot. Using a rice paddle, gently fluff the rice, mix in the butter, and break up the scallops after sliding in the butter.
6. After adding the finely chopped chives, serve right away. This dish of rice with scallops is deliciously served on its own or as a "fancy rice" side dish to a more substantial meal.

63. RICE COOKER VEGETABLE THAI CURRY

Prep Time: 15 Minutes | Cook Time: 40 Minutes

Total Time: 55 Minutes | Serving: 3-4

Ingredients

- 3 tbsp Thai red or yellow curry paste
- 1 tbsp fish sauce
- 1 small onion, chopped
- 1 cup of water
- 1 cup of coconut milk
- 1 cup of snow peas
- 1 tbsp brown sugar
- 1 medium carrot, peeled and chopped
- 1 red bell pepper, seeded and chopped
- 1 ½ cup of chopped broccoli

Instructions

1. Once the rice cooker's inner pot is filled with onion, carrot, bell pepper, snow peas, curry paste, water, and sugar, select the [Slow Cook] setting. Assign a 40-minute time slot.
2. In the final ten minutes of simmering, add the broccoli, coconut milk, and fish sauce. Make sure to thoroughly mix before serving.

64. RICE COOKER CHICKEN AND SAUSAGE JAMBALAYA

Prep Time: 10 Minutes | Cook Time: 45 Minutes

Total Time: 55 Minutes | Serving: 6-8

Ingredients

- 3 green onions, sliced
- 3 cups of chicken broth
- 1 red bell pepper, diced
- 1/4 tsp pepper
- 1 small onion, diced
- 2 cups of cooked shredded chicken
- 3 tbsp butter
- 1/4 cup of chopped fresh parsley
- 2-3 cloves garlic, minced
- 13.5ounces andouille sausage, sliced
- 1 tsp Creole or Cajun seasoning
- 1 1/2 cups of white rice

Instructions

1. Warm the butter in a big frying pan over medium-high heat. Put the onion and pepper, and cook for three to five minutes or until soft. When everything is nicely browned, add the sausage and garlic.
2. Pour the broth and rice into the rice cooker. Stir in the sausage and sauteed veggies, then add the chicken. Mix thoroughly after adding the pepper and spice.
3. Place the rice cooker on the "cook" setting. Serve the rice right away after adding the parsley and green onions.

65. RICE COOKER HAINANESE CHICKEN RICE

Prep Time: 5 Minutes | Cook Time: 20 Minutes

Total Time: 25 Minutes | Serving: 4

Ingredients

- scallions for garnish
- 2 Tbsp sesame oil
- 6 chicken drumsticks approx 1 1/2 pounds
- 2 cups of rice uncooked
- 1/2 inch of ginger cut into thin strips
- 3 cloves garlic chopped
- 1 dash ground black pepper
- 3 cups of chicken stock
- 3 pandan leaves tied into a knot (optional)
- Hot sauce recommended: sriracha or sambal oelek for serving

Instructions

1. Apply sesame oil to the drumsticks of chicken. Add a dash of black pepper on top. Give it a good 20 minutes to marinade. After washing, drain the rice. Place inside the rice cooker.
2. Add the pandan leaves, ginger, and garlic to the chicken stock (fill your rice cooker to the 2-cup of mark). Over the rice, arrange the chicken drumsticks.
3. Put the rice cooker on and allow it to cook.
4. After the rice cooker has finished cooking, take off the lid and let it another ten minutes or so. Take the chicken out of the rice cooker.
5. Use a fork or a pair of chopsticks to fluff the rice. Serve rice with hot sauce and chicken. Add scallions as a garnish.

66. SLOW COOKER CHICKEN CURRY

Prep Time: 5 Minutes | Cook Time: 4 Hour

Total Time: 4 Hour 5 Minutes | Serving: 6

Ingredients

- 1/2 tsp Salt
- 1/2 tsp Chilli flakes
- 3 tbsp Medium curry powder
- 100 g Mango chutney
- 1 tsp Garam Masala
- 400 ml Reduced fat Coconut Milk
- 1 kg Boneless, skinless chicken thighs
- 1 Large Onion, Peeled and very finely chopped, I use frozen ready prepared
- 4 Cloves Garlic, Peeled and chopped, or frozen, ready prepared
- 2 tsp Fresh ginger, Peeled and grated, or use a ready prepared paste

Instructions

1. Place all the ingredients in the slow cooker (crock pot) EXCEPT the garam masala. Stir it thoroughly.
2. Close the lid and bake for 4 hours on HIGH or 6 hours minimum on LOW.
3. Using two forks, gently shred the chicken until it's tender and coming apart, then add the Garam Masala. Stir everything thoroughly to coat and soften it in the sauce.

67. RICE COOKER GINGER CHICKEN AND RICE

Prep Time: 15 Minutes | Cook Time: 45 Minutes

Total Time: 1 Hour | Serving: 4

Ingredients

- 1 1/4 pounds skinless, boneless chicken thighs, cut into 1-inch cubes
- Kosher salt
- 3 packed cups of baby spinach
- One 2-inch piece of fresh ginger, peeled and cut into matchsticks
- 3/4 cup of hot water
- 1 cup of unsweetened coconut milk
- 1 large chicken bouillon cube, preferably all-natural
- 1 cup of jasmine rice

Instructions

1. The bouillon cube should dissolve in the boiling water in a small bowl. Add the rice, ginger, and chicken to a rice cooker. Spread the spinach over the top. Add the coconut milk and broth from the bouillon to the cooker, then lightly season with salt. After the cooker automatically shuts off, the meal should be done in approximately 40 minutes. Give it a five-minute wait. Using a fork, fluff the rice, transfer it to bowls, and then serve.

68. CREAMY CAJUN CHICKEN PASTA

Prep Time: 10 Minutes | Cook Time: 20 Minutes

Total Time: 30 Minutes | Serving: 6

Ingredients

- ♦ 1 1/2 cup of heavy whipping cream
- ♦ 1 1/2 to 2 Tbsp cajun seasoning, divided
- ♦ 3 garlic cloves, minced
- ♦ 1/2 cup of grated parmesan cheese
- ♦ 2 Tbsp unsalted butter
- ♦ 2/3 cup of diced tomatoes
- ♦ 2 boneless skinless chicken breasts
- ♦ 8 ounce linguine pasta
- ♦ 2 tsp olive oil
- ♦ 2 Tbsp parsley, finely chopped, to serve

Instructions

1. Add one tbsp of salt to a big saucepan of boiling water. Bake pasta as directed on the package until it's al dente. Set aside half a cup of pasta water, then cover, drain, and keep warm.
2. Even out the thickness of the chicken breasts by beating them, then sprinkle 1½ tbsp cajun seasoning over them all.
3. Warm up two tbsp of oil in a big, non-reactive skillet over medium-high heat. When it's heated, add the chicken and sear it all over. Reduce heat to low and saute until done, as measured by a thermometer reading of 165°F. After transferring to a chopping board, thinly slice and cover to maintain the warmth.
4. Put the garlic and butter in the same skillet and cook over medium flame for 30-60 seconds or until the garlic becomes fragrant. Saute for a further two minutes after adding the diced tomatoes.
5. Simmer after adding the heavy whipping cream, parmesan cheese, and any more cajun seasoning to taste. Add more seasoning to taste.
6. When the pasta and chicken are well heated, add the sliced chicken and cooked spaghetti to the sauce and toss again. If you want to thin the sauce, add the warmed pasta water that you saved. Add freshly grated Parmesan cheese and finely chopped parsley as garnish.

69. RICE COOKER CHICKEN

Prep Time: 10 Minutes | Cook Time: 45 Minutes | Additional Time: 1 Hour

Total Time: 1 Hour 55 Minutes | Serving: 4

Ingredients

- ♦ 4 boneless chicken thighs
- ♦ 1 cup of water, or as needed - divided
- ♦ 6 cloves garlic, smashed
- ♦ 1 ½ tsp cornstarch
- ♦ ½ cup of soy sauce
- ♦ ½ tsp sesame seed oil
- ♦ 4 slices fresh ginger root, coarsely chopped
- ♦ 1 tsp monosodium glutamate (such as Ac'cent®) (Optional)
- ♦ 1 tsp salt
- ♦ ½ tsp ground black pepper

Instructions

1. To dissolve the salt and stir the ingredients, place the sesame oil, soy sauce, ginger, garlic, and monosodium glutamate (if using) in a large resealable plastic bag. Squeeze the bag to mix the contents. To coat the chicken, add the marinated chicken thighs to the bag and squeeze it once more. After removing as much air as you can from the bag, zip it shut. Put in the fridge for one hour.

2. In a small bowl, mix cornstarch with two tbsp of water until smooth. Transfer the marinade from the plastic bag into an electric rice cooker with a preset function, then blend in the cornstarch mixture until well blended. Spoon the sauce over the chicken thighs. Stir the chicken and add just enough water to barely cover it.

3. After locking the cooker's cover, select the standard rice setting, then hit the start button. Once steam starts to emerge from the cooker's top, which should happen after approximately 20 minutes, program the timer for 10 minutes. After the timer sounds, uncover and give the chicken a stir. Put the cooker on the keep-warm setting after another ten minutes of cooking according to the timer. Before serving, let the chicken rest for 20 minutes on the keep-warm setting.

70. FRIED CHICKEN RICE

Prep Time: 5 Minutes | Cook Time: 15 Minutes

Total Time: 20 Minutes | Serving: 4

Ingredients

- 1 fried chicken drumstick
- 2 cups of (370 g) uncooked short-grain white rice
- 2 tbsp soy sauce
- 2 ½ cups of (592 ml) water

Instructions

1. After rinsing the rice until the majority of the water runs clear, thoroughly drain. To cook rice on a stovetop, add water, soy sauce, and rice to the rice cooker insert.
2. After centering the fried chicken drumstick in the rice, switch on the rice cooker.
3. When rice is cooked, take out the chicken, chop it small, shred it, and then stir it back into the rice. Furikake is optionally served on top.

71. CREAM CORN CHICKEN RICE

Prep Time: 10 Minutes | Cook Time: 20 Minutes

Total Time: Minutes | Serving: 3-4

Ingredients

- 2 x 398ml / 14 fl. ounce cans of cream style corn
- 2-3 dashes white pepper powder
- ¼ tsp salt
- High heat oil for cooking
- ½ tsp soy sauce
- 1 pound ground chicken
- 1 garlic clove, peeled
- 1 tbsp Chinese cooking wine
- 1/8 tsp curry powder
- 1 tsp toasted sesame oil
- Splash of broth or water, as needed to thin to desired consistency

To serve:

- Drizzle more toasted sesame oil
- Scallions for garnish
- Steamed white rice

Instructions

1. Over medium-high heat, preheat a large skillet. Add the ground chicken after adding around two tsp of oil after it's heated. Using a spatula, break separate clumps. I minced the garlic clove in the garlic press and then added it to the pan without using my knife or chopping board. Grate your garlic using a knife if you don't have a press. Curry powder, white pepper powder, and salt should be added. Cook for twenty seconds. If it's getting too hot, turn the heat down to medium. When most of the alcohol scent has dissipated, add the cooking wine and saute for an additional 20 seconds.
2. Add the cream-style corn and cook until heated through. Incorporate the toasted sesame oil and soy sauce. Put a splash of water or broth, depending on your preference, for a little thinner consistency. As necessary, adjust the seasonings (soy sauce, sesame oil, and salt) based on taste. Alongside white rice, serve. If desired, add a drizzle more of the sesame oil. Add scallions on top. Enjoy yourself!

72. RICE COOKER SPANISH CHICKEN RICE

Prep Time: 5 Minutes | Cook Time: 20 Minutes

Total Time: 25 Minutes | Serving: 6

Ingredients

- 400g canned chopped tomatoes
- 2 tbs butter
- 1 1/2 cups of Massel Chicken Style Liquid Stock
- 1 brown onion (diced,medium)
- 1/2 cup of parsley (chopped)
- 600g chicken tenderloins
- 1 1/2 cups of rice
- 3 garlic cloves (sliced)
- 1 tsp ground cumin

Instructions

1. Put the butter, onion, and garlic into the rice cooker and set it to a high temperature. The onion should be sauteed until transparent.
2. Stir in the rice, tomatoes, stock, and ground cumin. Place the tenderloins of chicken on top.
3. Cook with a cover on for 20 minutes. With an automatic rice cooker, you might need to hit the cook button a few times.
4. After removing the tenderloins, chop them, add them back to the pot, and gently stir to mix in the chopped parsley.

73. RICE COOKER CHICKEN & SOY SAUCE RICE

Prep Time: 10 Minutes | Cook Time: 30 Minutes

Total Time: 40 Minutes | Serving: 2

Ingredients

- ♦ 3g ginger, julienned
- ♦ black pepper to taste
- ♦ 12g garlic, minced
- ♦ 2 boneless chicken thighs
- ♦ 3 tbsp low-sodium soy sauce
- ♦ 1 tsp dark soy sauce
- ♦ 3 tbsp oyster sauce

Rice:

- ♦ 1 cup of salted chicken broth
- ♦ 1 cup of short or medium grain rice, uncooked

Scallion & ginger sauce:

- ♦ neutral oil
- ♦ very finely minced scallions (whites and greens)
- ♦ salt to taste
- ♦ very finely minced ginger

Other:

- ♦ steamed broccolini
- ♦ scallions for garnish

Instructions

1. To begin, season the chicken with oyster sauce, dark soy sauce, soy sauce, minced garlic, and julienned ginger. Using your hands, thoroughly mix and leave aside.
2. After giving the rice multiple rinses in cool water until the water is reasonably clear, drain the entire amount of water. Top the rice with the chicken thighs and pour in the seasoned chicken broth. Ensure that any leftover sauce is scraped into the rice cooker and over the chicken.
3. While the rice cooker is heating up, prepare the scallion and ginger sauce. To toast the aromatics, you can heat the oil, but for a cleaner, more pure flavor, I like to add the oil right from the bottle. The most crucial piece of advice is to mince the ginger and scallions for a better texture.
4. Before plating, remove the chicken and slice. After that, fluff the rice and serve it with the dipping sauce made of garlic and scallions, along with some steamed broccolini.

74. LEMON CHICKEN AND RICE

Prep Time: 10 Minutes | Cook Time: 35 Minutes

Total Time: 45 Minutes | Serving: 4

Ingredients

Chicken:

- ♦ Salt and pepper
- ♦ 1 tsp Italian seasoning
- ♦ 1 lemon, sliced
- ♦ 4 chicken thighs, (skin on, bone in)
- ♦ 2 tbsp butter

Rice:

- ♦ ½ tsp salt
- ♦ 1 tsp garlic powder
- ♦ 1 red onion, chopped
- ♦ 1 cup of white rice, (uncooked)
- ♦ 4 garlic cloves, minced
- ♦ 1 tsp Italian seasoning
- ♦ 2 ¼ cups of chicken broth
- ♦ Parsley , (for garnish)

Instructions

Chicken:

1. Give the chicken a dose of salt, pepper, and Italian spice. After preheating the skillet to medium-high heat, add the butter. After it has melted, add the seasoned chicken to the skillet and cook over medium-high flame for 5 minutes on each side.
2. Once the chicken is out of the pan, add the lemons. Just slightly sear them to release the juices. Lemons should also be taken out of the pan.

Rice:

1. Slightly transparent onion and garlic should be added to the same skillet and cooked.
2. In a saucepan over medium flame, combine the rice, chicken broth, salt, garlic powder, and Italian seasoning. Use a wooden spoon and scrape the pan to get rid of any burnt parts. After bringing the rice to a mild boil, simmer it.
3. To make the rice tender and the liquid absorbed, place the chicken on top of the rice, cover it with a lid, and boil for a further 20 to 25 minutes.
4. Remember to use a knife to check the doneness of the chicken. Just before the chicken is done simmering, it should be fully cooked.
5. Snoouncee the heat. When adding a lot of lemon zest, make sure the rice is well combined. Close the lid and let it sit for roughly five minutes. Add some parsley as garnish.

75. CHICKEN AND RICE CASSEROLE

Prep Time: 10 Minutes | Cook Time: 2 Hour

Total Time: 2 hour 10 Minutes | Serving: 6

Ingredients

- 2 cups of water
- cooking spray
- 1 can cream of mushroom soup
- 1 can cream of celery soup
- 1 tsp paprika regular or smoked paprika
- 6 bone-in skin-on chicken pieces such as legs, thighs or drumsticks
- 1 can cream of chicken soup
- salt and pepper to taste
- 3 tbsp butter melted
- 2 tbsp chopped parsley
- 2 cups of white rice

Instructions

1. Pour in the three soup cans, water, and rice. Toss to mix.
2. Layer the rice mixture with the chicken pieces on top. Brush the chicken and rice with a little butter.
3. Apply salt, pepper, and paprika to the chicken to season it.
4. Bake for one and a half hours with the foil covering you. The fridge temperature should be raised to 400 degrees.
5. After the chicken has browned and all of the liquid has been absorbed, take the lid and continue baking for another 20-30 minutes. Bake the dish for 3 to 5 minutes, or until the chicken skin is particularly crispy if you want that. After serving, add a little parsley.

76. PESTO CHICKEN AND RICE BAKE

Prep Time: 10 Minutes | Cook Time: 45 Minutes

Total Time: 55 Minutes | Serving: 4

Ingredients

- 1 (6.9 ounce) package chicken-flavored rice and vermicelli mix
- 1 pound chicken tenderloins, tendons removed, cut into smaller pieces if desired
- ¼ cup of freshly grated Parmesan cheese
- 1 ¾ cups of water, divided
- ½ cup of Alfredo sauce
- cooking spray
- 4 tbsp basil pesto, divided

Instructions

1. Set the oven's temperature to 375°F, or 190°C. Apply cooking spray to an 8-inch casserole dish.
2. Combine rice, seasoning packets, 1 1/2 cups of water, and two tbsp pesto. Fill the prepared casserole dish with the ingredients.
3. In a shallow bowl, toss the chicken tenders with the remaining two tbsp of pesto. Put the chicken over the rice.
4. Cook for thirty minutes in a preheated oven. When placed in the center, an instant-read thermometer should read at least 165 degrees F.
5. Mix the Alfredo sauce with the remaining 1/4 cup of water. After taking the baking dish out of the oven, cover the chicken with the Alfredo sauce and swirl to mix. Sprinkle Parmesan cheese on top, then bake for a further 15 minutes or until the cheese melts. Serve right away.

77. CRISPY SESAME CHICKEN AND GINGER RICE

Prep Time: 15 Minutes | Cook Time: 15 Minutes

Total Time: 30 Minutes | Serving: 6

Ingredients

- kosher salt and black pepper
- 6 tbsp extra virgin olive oil or sesame oil
- 4 cloves garlic, grated
- 1/2 cup of pomegranate juice
- 2 tbsp honey
- 1/4 cup of all-purpose flour (or gluten free all-purpose flour)
- 1 1/2 pounds boneless chicken breasts, cut into 2 inch cubes
- 2 cups of broccoli florets

- 1 bay leaf
- 2 tbsp rice vinegar
- 1 tbsp fresh grated ginger
- 1 tsp crushed red pepper flakes, use more or less to taste
- 1/4 cup of toasted sesame seeds
- 1 star anise
- 2 shallots, sliced
- 1 egg, beaten
- 1/3 cup of low sodium soy sauce
- green onions, for serving

Instructions

1. Warm up the oven to 475°F. Use parchment paper or oil to coat a baking sheet.
2. Place the chicken in a bowl with the egg and a dash of pepper. Mix by tossing. Pour the flour into a different bowl. In batches, coat the chicken by dredging it in flour and tossing it. After the baking sheet is ready, place the chicken on one side. Pour in two tbsp of oil. On the opposite side of the pan, add the broccoli and shallots. Toss with two additional tbsp of oil, salt, and pepper. Bake for a duration of 12 minutes. When the chicken is cooked through, toss in the broccoli, turn it over, and put it back in the oven for a further three to five minutes.
3. Meanwhile, put the rice vinegar, honey, pomegranate juice, star anise, bay leaf, garlic, ginger, and red pepper flakes in a big skillet. Place the pan over medium-high heat and boil the sauce. Boil the sauce for 5 to 8 minutes or until it thickens and reduces by around one-third. Add the broccoli, chicken, and sesame seeds and stir. Cook the chicken until it is covered with sauce.
4. Over bowls of ginger rice, sprinkle with green onions, and arrange the chicken, broccoli, and sauce.

78. CHICKEN AND MUSHROOM RICE

Prep Time: 20 Minutes | Cook Time: 45 Minutes

Total Time: 1 Hour 5 Minutes | Serving: 4

Ingredients

- 6 dried shiitake mushrooms, thinly sliced
- 2 chicken thighs (230 gm), cut into thin strips
- 1/2 onion finely chopped
- 2 cups of white rice
- 1 spring onion / scallions, finely chopped

Stock:

- 1 tsp sugar
- 750 ml low sodium chicken stock
- 1 tsp ginger, finely grated
- 1 tbsp oyster sauce
- 1/2 tbsp soy sauce

Marinade:

- 1 tbsp honey
- cracked pepper, to taste
- 1 tbsp soy sauce

Optional Extras:

- steamed broccoli
- steamed Asian greens
- steamed beans

Instructions

1. After soaking the mushrooms for twenty minutes in a bowl of recently boiled water, thinly slice them.
2. Rinse the rice in the rice cooker bowl with cold tap water about three times, then drain. Mix thoroughly after adding the stock components.
3. Press the rice cooker's Start button after adding the chopped onions and a piece of mushrooms to the rice. Keep still. (Usually takes thirty to forty minutes.)
4. Slice the chicken into thin pieces. Place the ingredients for the marinade in a bowl and stir until the rice is cooked.
5. When the rice is cooked, fluff it up briefly with a spoon before sealing the cover. To prevent the rice from burning, be careful to fluff the rice at the bottom of the dish.
6. Without adding too much marinade, quickly arrange the marinated chicken strips over the rice. After closing the lid and pressing the "cook" button once more, let the steam run for ten to twelve minutes.
7. Verify that the chicken pieces are done after ten minutes. If they're still raw, cover and continue cooking until they're done. After cooking, give the rice another stir and serve.

79. CHICKEN CONGEE

Prep Time: 10 Minutes | Cook Time: 25 Minutes

Total Time: 35 Minutes | Serving: 2

Ingredients

- 900ml water
- 4 slices ginger
- 11/2tsp salt, or to taste
- 100g long grain rice
- 1 chicken breast, cubed
- 25g dried scallops (optional)

To garnish:

- 1 spring onion, sliced
- White pepper

Instructions

1. Wash the rice in the basin of the rice cooker. It may take three to four times to get the water completely clear after washing and draining it frequently.
2. Assemble the spring onions, ginger, and chicken breast.
3. Soak the dried scallops in a dish of warm water to prepare them. After 30 seconds, use your hands to tear them apart so that strips are obtained.
4. Add water to the rice in the rice cooker bowl. Next, include the chicken, dried scallops, and ginger. Shut the cover.
5. Simmer for twenty-five minutes. To test the consistency, stir it. There shouldn't be much water remaining, so it should feel quite runny. If it's excessively runny, wait three more minutes before checking. If it becomes too thick, add a little water, stir, and let it sit for three more minutes to reheat.
6. To taste, add salt. Add some spring onions and a dash of white pepper as garnish.

80. SEA BREAM RICE

Prep Time: 10 Minutes | Cook Time: 50 Minutes

Total Time: 1 Hour | Serving: 3

Ingredients

- ◆ 1 dash Salt
- ◆ 1 tbsp Soy sauce
- ◆ 1 tbsp Sake
- ◆ 1 whole fish Sea bream
- ◆ 1 Kombu for dashi stock

Instructions

1. Take off the fish's scales, take out its insides, and wash the blood off. Thirty minutes before cooking, wash three cups of rice and drain in a sieve. After adding salt, let the fish sit for about half an hour. Grill until both sides are singed.
2. In the rice cooker, place the rinsed and drained rice. To make three cups, add the sake, soy sauce, and water. Mix in a small pinch of salt, then place the kombu on top. Place the fish on top and cook.
3. After the rice is cooked, remove the fish and kombu and let it sit and steam for ten minutes or so. Fish should be deboned, flaked, and returned to the rice cooker. Stir into the rice.

81. LEMON DILL RICE

Prep Time: 5 Minutes | Cook Time: 20 Minutes

Total Time: 25 Minutes | Serving: 4-6

Ingredients

- 3 cups of chicken or vegetable broth
- 1/2 tsp kosher salt
- 1 1/2 cups of basmati or long grain rice
- 1 large shallot, finely minced
- 3 tbsp lemon juice
- 2 tbsp unsalted butter or olive oil
- 1/4 tsp freshly cracked pepper
- 1 tbsp lemon zest
- 1/3 cup of minced fresh dill

Instructions

1. In a large skillet over a medium flame, melt the butter or olive oil. When the shallot is softened, saute it for two to three minutes.
2. Toss the rice in the pan with the butter/olive oil and shallot to coat it. Stirring often, cook the rice for two to three minutes. Simmer after adding the broth, lemon zest, salt, and pepper.
3. Cook for 20 minutes with a lid on and low heat. Once the pan has cooked for 20 minutes, take it off the heat and leave it covered for an additional 10 minutes.
4. After fluffing the rice, mix in the fresh dill and lemon juice. To taste, add more pepper and salt to season.

82. SIMPLE SHRIMP AND ASPARAGUS RISOTTO

Prep Time: 15 Minutes | Cook Time: 45 Minutes

Total Time: 1 Hour| Serving: 4

Ingredients

- 16 jumbo shrimp (16/20 count), peeled and deveined
- salt and freshly cracked black pepper
- 1 cup of freshly grated parmesan cheese
- 1 cup of asparagus chopped into 1" pieces
- 1-1/2 cups of arborio rice
- 1 shallot, minced
- 6 cups of chicken stock
- 4 Tbsp butter
- 1/2 cup of dry white wine (pinot grigio or sauvignon blanc recommended)
- 4 cloves garlic, pressed or minced

Instructions

1. Remove the chicken stock from the burner and cover the pot to keep it warm. Place it over high heat in a medium saucepan.
2. Over medium flame, melt butter in a large 11- to 12-inch skillet. Add shallot and saute for 2 to 3 minutes or until softened. Once the garlic is aromatic, add it and saute it for an additional minute.
3. Stir in the rice, then simmer, stirring, for one minute to coat it in butter. The rice will absorb the wine almost immediately after adding it, so mix gently and constantly. When the rice is almost completely absorbed, add 1/2 cup (one ladleful) of chicken stock and stir continually. Once the stock has almost been absorbed by the rice, add another 1/2 cup of or 1 ladleful at a time, stirring carefully and constantly.
4. Add the asparagus and stir-fry it for another three to four additions remaining in the stock. Add shrimp and stir-fry until the rice is soft and the shrimp are cooked through, using about two additions of liquid total. This should take about thirty to forty minutes to complete. It's acceptable if the rice is perfectly soft before the last of the stock is added. Only some things have to be added.
5. Remove the heat source, stir in the parmesan cheese, and put salt and pepper to taste. Present right away.

83. SPICY TUNA SUSHI BOWL WITH CRISPY RICE

Prep Time: 10 Minutes | Cook Time: 10 Minutes

Total Time: 20 Minutes | Serving: 1

Ingredients

- 1 tbsp sriracha
- 1 cup of cooked sushi rice, chilled
- 2 tsp soy sauce
- 1/4 cup of scallions, chopped
- 1 tbsp avocado oil or another heat-tolerant oil
- 2 tbsp mayonnaise
- 1 mini cucumber, sliced
- 1/2 tsp toasted sesame oil
- 1/2 tsp rice wine vinegar
- 1 (5 ounce) can tuna (preferably oil-packed), drained
- Sesame seeds, chili crisp and nori sheets for serving (optional)

Instructions

1. Combine the canned tuna, soy sauce, vinegar, sriracha, mayonnaise, and toasted sesame oil to produce the spicy tuna. Store in the fridge until needed.
2. Before adding the avocado oil, heat a big skillet over medium-high heat for a few minutes. Whenever the oil begins to shimmer, add the rice in big clusters and press down hard with a spatula. Cook for three to five minutes or until golden brown and crispy.
3. Add a scoop of spicy tuna, crispy rice pieces, cucumber, and sesame seeds, along with a drizzle of chili crisp, to construct the bowls.

84. QUICK THAI FISH CURRY & COCONUT RICE

Prep Time: 15 Minutes | Cook Time: 15 Minutes

Total Time: 30 Minutes | Serving: 6-8

Ingredients

- 2 limes, divided
- 2 Tbsp avocado oil
- 1 Tbsp fish sauce
- 4 tsp Thai Spice Blend, divided
- 1 bunch of baby kale or a couple handfuls of baby greens (kale, chard, spinach)
- 1 - 1 1/2 pounds thick white fish (like halibut, cod, or rockfish)
- Sriracha or sambal oelek (optional)
- 1/4 cup of coconut oil or more avocado oil
- 1 recipe Instant Pot Coconut Rice
- 1 - 13.5 ounce can of coconut milk
- 1 tsp sea salt

Instructions

1. Once the curry is done, start your Instant Pot Coconut Rice (or Jasmine Rice or any other type of rice you're making).
2. Arrange the fish onto a sizable platter or a compact baking dish. If the fillets are lengthy, cut them in half so that they all fit in the skillet.
3. Over the fish, evenly distribute 1/2 tsp salt and 1 tsp Thai Spice Blend. After turning the fillets over, sprinkle the remaining 1/2 tsp and one tsp of Thai spice on the other side. Drizzle the fish with two tbsp of avocado oil and squeeze one lime juice. To ensure that they are evenly covered in oil, citrus, and spices, flip them over a couple of times. Before cooking, let them settle for 10 to 15 minutes (or refrigerate for up to 2 hours).
4. In a big skillet, flame the coconut oil over high heat. The fish should not cook through at this time; instead, heat for a few minutes on each side until lightly browned, and then return to the dish or pan.
5. Toss in the can of coconut milk and the kale or greens (be careful; it will sear). You can assist the coconut milk in deglazing the pan by scraping the bottom to get rid of any trapped fish pieces. Add the fish sauce, the remaining two tsp of Thai spice, the juice from one lime, and a squeeze or two of Sriracha (if using).
6. After adding the fish back to the skillet, heat it for about five minutes or until the fish is cooked through and the sauce is thickened. Taste and adjust the seasoning with a little salt if desired.
7. Spoon a portion of rice, a fish fillet, some sauce, and greens into each bowl. If preferred, top with a splash of Sriracha and serve.

85.SHRIMP AND ANDOUILLE SAUSAGE JAMBALAYA

Prep Time: 10 Minutes | Cook Time: 40 Minutes

Total Time: 50 Minutes | Serving: 8

Ingredients

- 1 bay leaf
- 2 cups of chopped yellow onion
- 1/2 cup of chopped scallions
- 1/2 tsp cayenne pepper
- 1/2 cup of chopped celery
- 1 tsp paprika
- 1 pound large raw shrimp
- 4 cups of chicken stock + 1 cup of water rinsed from the carton
- 1 cup of chopped bell pepper

- 14.5 ounce can fire roasted tomatoes
- 2 tbsp neutral cooking oil
- 1 tbsp minced garlic
- freshly ground black pepper
- 2 cups of long-grain white rice rinsed for about 1 minute until the water runs clear
- 12 ounces smoked andouille sausage sliced into 1/4 inch rounds
- 1/2 tsp dried oregano
- salt

Instructions

1. Heat the oil in a big, wide saucepan (I used a 5-quart braiser, but you could use a large soup pot) over medium to medium-high heat. Add the celery, onions, and peppers. Put 1/2 tsp salt and 1/4 tsp pepper for seasoning. Reduce heat and simmer until slightly tender, about 7 to 8 minutes.
2. When the sausage's flavor and fat have drained out and the veggies have become even more tender, add the sausage, paprika, cayenne, and oregano. Cook for an additional five minutes.
3. Mix for 30 seconds after adding the garlic, and then mix in the rice. Toasted the rice for three minutes with constant stirring.
4. Bring the mixture to a simmer; next, lower the flame to a simmer while adding the chicken stock, one cup of water, tomatoes, and bay leaf.
5. To prevent the rice from settling and burning on the bottom, simmer the pan with a cover-on for 15 to 20 minutes while stirring from time to time.
6. Once the rice has absorbed most of the liquid and is almost soft, add the shrimp and scallions, place a lid on it, and turn off the heat. For a further five minutes, leave the pan on the burner to cook the shrimp gradually. It's time to serve and savor the jambalaya!

86. SEARED SCALLOPS WITH CITRUS-GINGER QUINOA

Prep Time: 20 Minutes | Cook Time: 5 Minutes | Additional Time: 15

Total Time: 40 Minutes | Serving: 4

Ingredients

- 1 pound fresh or frozen sea scallops
- 4 tsp butter
- ¼ tsp salt
- ½ cup of quinoa, rinsed and drained
- ½ tsp finely shredded lemon peel, divided
- ¾ tsp finely shredded orange peel, divided
- ½ cup of reduced-sodium chicken broth
- 1 cup of water
- 2 tbsp chopped fresh basil
- 4 leaves Fresh basil leaves
- 1 tsp grated fresh ginger
- ¼ tsp crushed red pepper

Instructions

1. Shake off any frozen scallops. Wash the scallops and use paper towels to pat dry. Put aside.
2. In a small saucepan, mix together the water, quinoa, ginger, 1/2 tsp of shredded orange peel, 1/4 tsp of shredded lemon peel, salt, and crushed red pepper. Boil, then turn down the heat. Boil, covered, until liquid is absorbed, about 15 minutes. Add chopped basil and stir.
3. Meanwhile, heat a big skillet over medium-high heat to melt butter. Scallops should be added to the skillet. Cook for 2-3 minutes, flipping once or until scallops are almost opaque. Lift the scallops out of the skillet and reserve. Pour the broth into the skillet along with the leftover 1/4 tsp of shredded orange and 1/4 tsp of shredded lemon peel. Heat till boiling. Boil for two minutes, uncovered.
4. Over the quinoa mixture, serve the scallops and broth combination. Add basil leaves as a garnish if you'd like.

87. THAI BASIL SHRIMP FRIED RICE

Prep Time: 15 Minutes | Cook Time: 10 Minutes

Total Time: 25 Minutes | Serving: 1

Ingredients

For the Sauce:

- 3 TBLS Oyster Sauce
- 1 TSP White Sugar
- 1 TBLS Water (or chicken broth or stock)
- 2 TSP Light Soy Sauce (preferably a Thai one or a low sodium light soy sauce)
- 1 TSP Sweet Dark Soy Sauce
- 1 TSP Fish Sauce

For the Thai Basil Shrimp Fried Rice:

- 2 TBLS Canola Oil
- 6 – 10 fresh Red Chilies
- 2 – 6 fresh Green chilies
- 1 small Yellow Onion – sliced into ¼-inch wide pieces
- 6 Garlic cloves – peeled, roughly chopped

To Serve:

- Reserved slices of large red chili, sliced cucumber, chopped fresh chilies in fish sauce
- 1.5cups of Thai Holy Basil Leaves
- 1 Large Red Chili (mild) – destemmed, deseeded if desired, thinly sliced at an angle
- 3 cups of cooked Long Grain Brown Rice
- 200 grams / 7 ounces peeled and deveined Shrimp

Instructions

1. Make the sauce: In a small measuring cup or bowl, whisk together oyster sauce, light soy sauce, sweet dark soy sauce, fish sauce, white sugar, and water until thoroughly blended.
2. Get the fresh ingredients ready. As directed in the "ingredients" section, prepare the garlic, huge red chile, green and red chilies, and yellow onion. Crush the garlic and fresh red and green chilies (not the sliced large red chili) into a coarse pulp with a mortar and pestle. Remove the holy basil leaves from the stems, rinse, and use paper towels to pat dry. After giving the shrimp a good rinse, pat dry.

For the Thai Basil Shrimp Fried Rice:

1. Heat two tbsp of canola oil in a big wok over a high flame and stir-fry the onion and aromatics. Put the onion and stir-fry for 20 seconds when it's heated. Stir-fry for 30 seconds to incorporate the large red chile and the smashed garlic chili paste, setting aside a few pieces for garnish. (Note: If necessary, open a window or turn on the exhaust fan. Chilies stir-fried over high heat can release strong odors and a lot of smoke.)
2. Cook the shrimp: Put the shrimp and stir-fry for one minute or until they are almost done and beginning to take on color.
3. Place the cooked brown rice in a bowl and cover with the sauce. Stir-fry for approximately a minute or until the sauce is fully mixed and every grain of rice is coated equally.
4. Stir in the basil: Include the holy basil leaves and stir just long enough to wilt them, around 30 seconds. Turn off the heating system.
5. To serve, move the mixture to a platter or divide it evenly among bowls, then top with the large red chili slices that were set aside. Or, for a more elegant presentation, put two of the huge red chili slices that were set aside in a dish and cover the contents with the fried rice. Using the back of a spoon, press down until the rice is evenly distributed. Spoon onto a dish. Continue this process with the remaining fried rice portions. If preferred, present the dish alongside sliced cucumber and finely chopped fresh chilies combined with fish sauce (prik nam pla) in a small bowl or sauce dish.

88. QUICK AND EASY PAELLA

Prep Time: 15 Minutes | Cook Time: 55 Minutes

Total Time: 1 Hour 10 Minutes | Serving: 6

Ingredients

Saffron Broth:

- ½ tsp saffron threads
- 1 pound jumbo shrimp, peeled and deveined, shells reserved
- 2 ¼ cups of chicken broth
- 2 tsp olive oil

Paella:

- 1 ⅓ cups of Arborio rice
- 1 tbsp olive oil
- ½ cup of green peas
- 8 ounces chorizo sausage, sliced into thin rounds
- 1 red bell pepper, cut into thin strips
- 1 pinch cayenne pepper, or more to taste
- 2 cloves garlic, minced
- 1 tsp paprika
- salt to taste
- ½ yellow onion, diced

Instructions

1. Reserved shrimp shells should be cooked and stirred for one to two minutes over medium heat in a pot with two tsp of olive oil or until the shells are pink and fragrant. Stir saffron into shells; pour in chicken broth; simmer for 20 minutes or until broth is aromatic and rusty colored.
2. Pass the saffron soup through a fine-mesh strainer; reserve 2 cups of the broth, transfer it to a small saucepan and keep it warm over low heat.
3. Turn the oven up to 425 F (220 C).
4. In a big ovenproof skillet, heat one tbsp of olive oil over medium heat. Fry chorizo slices in heated oil for two minutes on each side or until browned. Add onion to sausage and cook, stirring, for 3 minutes or until tender and starting to turn translucent. Switch to medium-low heat.
5. Add garlic to the chorizo mixture and stir-fry for about a minute or until fragrant. Stir the rice in the skillet until it is fully covered with oil, then add the peas.
6. Evenly pat the rice mixture into the skillet's bottom. Over the rice, arrange the shrimp in a single layer. Arrange the pepper strips between the shrimp and around them; sprinkle with cayenne, paprika, and salt.
7. Turn up the heat to high. Pour the reserved 2 cups of hot saffron broth over the shrimp as the rice starts to sizzle in the skillet, and shake the skillet slightly to ensure the liquid is well distributed.
8. For about 20 minutes, or when the rice is almost soft but still somewhat wet, bake the rice mixture in the preheated oven.

9. Set the pan over a medium-high flame and cook the rice for 3 to 5 minutes, or until it is tender, the liquid has been absorbed, and a small crust has formed on the bottom of the skillet from the caramelization of the rice.

89. ULTIMATE CORN AND CRAB BISQUE RECIPE

Prep Time: 5 Minutes | Cook Time: 25 Minutes

Total Time: 30 Minutes | Serving: 6

Ingredients

- ¾ tsp cayenne pepper
- 1 bay leaf
- ½ cup of chopped onion
- 4 tbsp unsalted butter
- 3 tbsp all-purpose flour
- 32 ounces seafood stock
- parsley optional, chopped for garnish

- 1 tsp ground black pepper
- 1 cup of half-and-half, divided
- 2 tsp creole or cajun seasoning
- ¼ cup of white wine
- 2 ears of fresh corn, cut off the cob
- 4 cloves garlic, chopped
- 1 pound fresh lump crab meat, picked over for shells
- ½ tsp kosher salt or to taste

Instructions

1. Place the crabmeat onto a sizable platter and feel the tender meat with your fingers. Aim to avoid breaking up any big lumps. Select and remove any cartilage or shell fragments; it's much simpler to feel than to see the fragments of the shell. Put aside.
2. In a big, heavy pot (a Dutch oven works well), melt the butter over medium flame. Put the onions and saute for about 5 minutes, or until they are transparent and soft after the butter has melted.
3. Add the black pepper, cayenne, garlic, bay leaf, and creole or cajun seasoning. Simmer and stir until the garlic begins to smell, which should take 30 to 60 seconds.
4. Pour in the seafood stock (or, if desired, chicken stock). Add the corn after bringing the liquid to a boil. After lowering the heat to low, cook for fifteen minutes.
5. Add the flour to half a cup of the half-and-half in a small bowl, and use a fork to stir until the mixture is lump-free and smooth. Add to the bisque mixture after that.
6. Pour in the remaining quarter cup of white wine and half of a cup of half-and-half. Turn up the heat to medium. Continue stirring until the bisque starts to get creamy and thick. It should take four to five minutes to complete.
7. Add the crab meat and turn the heat back down to low. Try not to break up the tiny lumps of crab by giving it a gentle stir. Cook until the bisque is heated, about 3 minutes.
8. If necessary, add a half tsp of kosher salt after tasting the soup. Serve right away after adding parsley as a garnish.

90. RICE COOKER CHINESE STICKY RICE

Prep Time: 20 Minutes | Cook Time: 25 Minutes

Total Time: 45 Minutes | Serving: 10

Ingredients

- 2-3 medium sized dried shiitake mushrooms
- 2 cups of Thai glutinous rice
- 1 ¼ cups of wate

- ¼ pound. (115g) shrimp, deveined and shells and tails removed
- 2 Chinese sausages
- ½ pound. (225g) ground pork

Sauce:

- ¼ tsp white pepper
- 3 tbsp oyster sauce
- 1 clove garlic, minced or grated
- 1 tbsp soy sauce

- 1 tsp grated ginger
- ½ tsp sesame oil
- ½ tsp tapioca starch

Instructions

1. After adding hot water to a bowl, add dry mushrooms and let soak for at least two hours or until mushy.
2. Pour cold water through a strainer filled with rice. Wash and rinse the rice thoroughly with a hand stir until the water runs mainly clear.
3. Give the rice at least two hours to soak in a bowl of water.
4. To prepare the sauce, combine, in a bowl, three tbsp oyster sauce, one tbsp soy sauce (or tamari), one tsp grated ginger, chopped garlic clove, ½ tsp tapioca starch, ½ tsp sesame oil, and ¼ tsp white pepper. Mix thoroughly. Put aside.
5. Remove the water from the rice by draining it through a colander.
6. Take the mushrooms out of the soaking mixture and use a soft spatula to extract some of the water. Trim and dispose of difficult stems. Slices or portions of mushroom tops should be cut. Cut Chinese sausages into round shapes.
7. In a skillet, preheat to medium. Cook the ground pork and Chinese sausage until the pork is almost done. Stir the sauce and mushrooms into the pan. Warm up thoroughly.
8. Remove from fire after adding the shrimp and cooking until they begin to turn pink.
9. Level out the rice cooker pot after transferring the Chinese sausage mixture to it.
10. Pour the drained rice on top and smooth it evenly. To the rice cooker, add a quarter cup of water.
11. Cook for around 25 minutes or until the rice cooker button pops. Give it another five to ten minutes. A hint of transparency and complete cooking are required for the rice.
12. Using chopsticks, fluff the rice and thoroughly mix it with the filling ingredients. If desired, garnish with finely sliced green onions.

91. CHICKEN RICE WITH VEGETABLES

Prep Time: 30 Minutes | Cook Time: 30 Minutes

Total Time: 1 Hour | Serving: 2

Ingredients

- 2 Chicken thighs bone-in small or boneless large
- Salt to taste and other spices or herbs as desired
- 1 1/2 cup of Rice uncooked, may mix with soaked whole grain rice varieties
- 2 cups of Choice of vegetable for steaming

Instructions

1. Sprinkle chicken thighs with salt and/or other spices and herbs, then let them sit for half an hour.
2. Rice should be rinsed with water to remove contaminants.
3. After adding water to fill the rice cooker to the 1 1/2 cup of level, put the raw rice in it.
4. Bake the rice with the pieces of chicken thighs on top.
5. After rinsing and preparing the veggies for steaming, chop them into small pieces.
6. When the rice has almost finished bubbling and absorbed all of the water, sprinkle the vegetables on top. Shut off the lid and carry on cooking.
7. Check the doneness of the chicken thighs with a fork or toothpick once the rice cooker is set to warm. The puncture should only be releasing clear liquid. Enjoy while warm!

92. PINEAPPLE TERIYAKI SALMON

Prep Time: 10 Minutes | Cook Time: 1 Hour

Total Time: 1 Hopur 10 Minutes | Serving: 2

Ingredients

- 2 cup of soy vey teriyaki
- 5 garlic cloves
- 3 scallions sliced on a bias for garnish
- 1/2 a pineapple diced up
- 2 pounds of wild salmon
- 1 inch piece of ginger
- juice and zest of one lemon

Instructions

1. Add the cubed pineapple, ginger, lemon juice, lemon zest, and good ole garlic. To blend, whisk vigorously! Additionally, remember to taste!
2. Cut the salmon into 4-ounce pieces and arrange them on a dish that is oven-safe.
3. Cover the fish with the teriyaki and pineapple sauce, then leave it for half an hour to an hour.
4. Place in a 450-degree preheated oven and cook for ten minutes.
5. Add the remaining pineapple dice and some sliced scallions as garnish.

93. RICE COOKER LENTILS

Prep Time: 10 Minutes | Cook Time: 30 Minutes

Total Time: 40 Minutes | Serving: 8

Ingredients

- 3 bay leaves
- 4 cups of No-Salt-Added Vegetable Stock
- 3 cloves garlic peeled
- 2 cups of lentils rinsed
- 1 tbsp olive oil

Instructions

1. After rinsing the lentils, remove any little stones or sticks.
2. Fill the rice cooker with lentils, water, bay leaves, olive oil, and garlic.
3. If you have a rice cooker, turn it on grain mode or close the top and cook on high.
4. After 40 minutes of cooking, make sure the lentils are done. If they require additional time, continue for ten more minutes and reevaluate. Continue every ten minutes until the lentils are cooked.

94. CLAY POT CHICKEN RICE IN RICE COOKER

Prep Time: 15 Minutes | Cook Time: 45 Minutes

Total Time: 1 Hour | Serving: 4

Ingredients

- 3 rehydrated dried shiitake mushrooms, thinly sliced
- 1 tsp sugar
- 1 tsp salt
- 4 tbsp oil
- 2 rice cooker cups of rice
- 1 inch ginger ,cut into 6 sliced
- 2 scallions , thinly sliced diagonally
- 2 Chinese sausages , thinly sliced diagonally
- 4 cloves garlic , minced
- 1 tsp sesame oil
- 450 gram (1 pound.) boneless skinless chicken thigh/breast
- enough water to cook rice according to your rice cooker
- 1/2 tsp ground white/black pepper

Marinating sauce:

- 1 tbsp dark soy sauce
- 1 tbsp light soy sauce
- 2 inch ginger, grated
- 1 tbsp oyster sauce

Instructions

1. Use the marinating sauce to coat the chicken breast, then refrigerate for fifteen minutes.
2. In a frying pan or wok with heated oil, saute the ginger and garlic for two to three minutes or until aromatic. Add all of the marinating sauce, the shiitake mushroom, the Chinese sausages, and the chicken cubes. Season with salt, sugar, and ground black and white pepper. Once the chicken is no longer pink, cook it.
3. When adding the rice to the skillet or wok, toss it thoroughly. It should be noted that the rice has not yet been cooked; instead, it has been combined with the other ingredients in the pan or wok. Pour the entire contents of the pan/wok into the pot of your rice cooker, add the water needed to cook the rice (according to the directions on your rice cooker), and then pour in the sesame oil.
4. Once the rice cooker reaches the "keep warm" stage, wait for fifteen minutes, then open the lid and add the sliced scallions. For more sophisticated models, use the "white rice" or "cook rice" feature. Using a paddle, fluff the rice and serve right away.

95. GROUND BEEF AND RICE

Prep Time: 10 Minutes | Cook Time: 35 Minutes

Total Time: 45 Minutes | Serving: 6

Ingredients

- 1 pound lean ground beef
- 2 cups of beef broth, I used a reduced sodium variety
- 1 cup of canned corn kernels
- 2 tsp olive oil
- 4 cloves garlic, minced
- 2 tsp chili powder
- ½ tsp ground cayenne pepper
- 1 tsp smoked paprika
- ½ tsp freshly ground black pepper
- 1 cup of chunky salsa
- 1 cup of canned black beans, rinsed and drained
- 1 tbsp butter
- ¾ tsp salt
- Chopped green onion, garnish to taste
- 1 cup of white basmati rice, rinsed and drained
- 1 tsp ground cumin
- Chopped grape or cherry tomatoes, garnish to taste
- 1 small yellow onion, peeled and diced

Instructions

1. Over medium flame, warm up the olive oil in a big saute pan. Incorporate the ground beef and allow it to cook for 8-10 minutes, stirring periodically and breaking it up into little bits as it cooks until it is thoroughly cooked.
2. With sporadic stirring, saute the onion and garlic with the ground beef for 3 to 5 minutes or until the onion has softened.
3. Black beans, rice, corn, salsa, butter, smoked paprika, cumin, cayenne, salt, and black pepper should all be added to the pan. Stir in the beef broth after combining everything.
4. Once boiling, lower the flame to a boil. Once the rice has absorbed the liquid and is cooked, cook it covered for 15 to 20 minutes.
5. Remember to keep cooking the rice; if it needs a little more time to cook, that's acceptable. You can add extra broth as needed.
6. Cook for 5 minutes, then cover and turn off the heat. Once the rice is fluffy, give everything a good toss. Top with green onions and tomatoes. Pour, then savor!

96. HAINANESE CHICKEN RICE IN RICE COOKER

Prep Time: 30 Minutes | Cook Time: 30 Minutes

Total Time: 1 Hour | Serving: 4

Ingredients

Chicken rice:

- 2 tbsp sesame oil, divided
- 3 cloves garlic, bruised
- 1 tsp salt
- 4 chicken drumsticks
- 1 inch ginger, grated
- 1/2 inch ginger, bruised

- 3 scallions, 2-inch pieces, thinly sliced
- 2 rice cooker cup (1 1/2 regular cup, or 300 gram) rice,
- 1 1/2 regular cup of (350 ml) chicken stock
- 3 cloves garlic, grated

Garlic ginger chili sauce:

- 1 inch ginger (~ 30 gram)
- 8-12 bird-eye red chilies
- 2 tbsp rice vinegar
- 5 cloves garlic

- 2 tbsp lime juice
- 1 tsp salt, or to taste
- 4 tbsp chicken stock
- 1/2 tbsp sugar, or to taste

Soy sauce for chicken:

- 2 tbsp water

- 2 tbsp light soy sauce

Instructions

1. Combine salt, a tbsp of sesame oil, sliced scallions, grated ginger, and grated garlic to marinate chicken drumsticks.
2. Before draining, rinse the rice several times under cold tap water until the water runs clean. In a frying pan, heat up roughly a tbsp of sesame oil and gently saute some ginger and garlic until aromatic.
3. Add the marinated chicken drumsticks, fried garlic, ginger, and rice to the rice cooker pot. Cover with chicken stock.
4. Use the standard "white rice" cooking setting. For the simplest rice cooker, use the "cook" setting. Once the light has switched to "keep warm," rest for a further fifteen minutes without lifting the rice cooker lid.
5. Once the rice cooker has cooked for fifteen minutes, uncover it, take out the chicken, fluff the rice, and place it in a serving dish. For chicken, serve with soy sauce and chili sauce. Process the red chilies, rice vinegar, ginger, garlic, sugar, salt, lime juice, and chicken stock in a food processor until smooth.
6. Mix light soy sauce and water to make soy sauce for the chicken.

97. RICE PUDDING IN A RICE COOKER

Prep Time: 20 Minutes | Cook Time: 45 Minutes

Total Time: 1 Hour 5 Minutes | Serving: 8

Ingredients

- ♦ 2 cups of short-grain rice,if using a reg measure cup use 1 1/2 cups
- ♦ 2 cups of cold water
- ♦ 3 tbsp ground cinnamon (to garnish)
- ♦ 1/2 cup of coconut milk
- ♦ 1 cup of sweetened condensed milk, Eagle Brand
- ♦ 1 lemon zest, one large piece of lemon peel
- ♦ 1/2 cup of evaporated milk
- ♦ 1 tsp salt
- ♦ 1/2 tsp nutmeg
- ♦ 1 cinnamon stick

Instructions

1. To measure your short grains, use the measuring cup of that comes with your rice cooker. Usually, this measuring cup holds six ounces or nearly three-quarters of a cup of rice. Two of those measures are where you need to start with this recipe.
2. Rice should be measured first, then rinsed in cold water. Then, the rice, water, and salt should be added to a rice cooker and turned on. Cook until the heated button appears on its own.
3. After cooking the rice and allowing it to cool for fifteen minutes, disconnect the cable from the outlet, stir the rice once, and adjust the temperature back to warm.
4. Concurrently, blend together coconut milk, sweetened condensed milk, cinnamon stick, nutmeg, and a large, thin piece of lemon zest—not the grated kind.
5. Once the milk has been stirred into the rice, cover the pot and turn the flame to WARM. Once half an hour has passed, check to see if the consistency is what you prefer.
6. Throw out the zest of the lemon and the cinnamon stick.
7. Spoon into separate servings and top with cream, if preferred, and crushed cinnamon.

98. RICE COOKER JAPANESE CHEESECAKE

Prep Time: 20 Minutes | Cook Time: 40 Minutes

Total Time: 1 Hour | Serving: 8

Ingredients

- 2 large eggs whites and yolks separated
- 2 tbsp lemon juice
- 40 grams cake flour approximately 5 tbsp
- 200 ml skim milk I made it with skim milk, but I think it should also work with low fat or whole
- 227 grams (8-ounce block) cream cheese softened
- 80 grams granulated sugar approximately 6 1/2 tbsp
- powdered sugar for dusting on top of the cake

Instructions

1. Put cream cheese in a large glass mixing bowl. Should your cream cheese be too firm, it won't incorporate well into the batter, resulting in small pieces of cream cheese. I suggest heating it in the microwave for 10-second intervals, covering the bowl's top with a paper towel in case it splatters until the cream cheese can be whisked into the consistency of creamy frosting.
2. Add egg yolks after the cream cheese has been whipped until it becomes smooth. Beat batter with a whisk until smooth. My experiments have taught me that it's crucial to blend everything until smooth after adding a new ingredient; otherwise, it will be quite difficult to get rid of the lumps later. Put the sugar and whisk until the batter is smooth. Lastly, blend the batter until it's smooth by adding the lemon juice.
3. Blend in the cake flour using a sieve. Sorting is a crucial step. The flour stays clumped if you add it in; even mixing it with an electric mixer didn't help the lumps go away.) Nevertheless, if you sift it in, whisking it into the batter requires a few whisks to make it smoothly mixed. Since I don't have a flour sifter, I pour the flour into a sieve and tap it gently against my other hand until all of the flour is filtered through. Sift flour into the batter and stir until smooth.
4. Smooth the batter with a gentle whisk after adding the milk.
5. Add the egg whites to a sanitized stand mixer bowl. To ensure that your egg whites whip properly, make sure that neither the egg whites nor the bowl have come into touch with any oils. Use a high-speed whisk to whip the egg whites until firm peaks form.

6. Beat in the egg whites in three batches into the batter. You don't want to beat out all the air you whipped into the egg whites, so gently fold them in after each addition. If the egg whites don't blend in entirely, that's acceptable. Once the egg whites are incorporated into the batter, there should still be some little egg white lumps and streaks.

7. Grease your rice cooker's interior thoroughly. For this recipe, I used a five 1/2 cup of rice cooker. Fill the pot with batter. Shut off the rice cooker and select "cake" from the menu. Select the white rice setting in your rice cooker if it doesn't have a cake function; you might need to press for a second cycle once the first one is through. Bake for approximately forty minutes. When the cooking time is almost up, you can open your rice cooker to see how the cake is doing. When you touch the cake, it should spring back and pull away from the rice cooker's sides. The surface should also have a uniformly cooked hue. Additionally, the size of your rice cooker will affect how long it takes to cook.

8. Carefully invert the rice cooker pot by placing a plate on top of it. The cake ought to fall naturally onto the plate. To allow the cheese flavor to fully develop and the cake to firm, place it in the refrigerator for at least an hour. The cake could be sweeter and will taste eggy if you try to eat it immediately. It tastes more sweeter and has more cheese flavor after it sets. When serving, dust with powdered sugar. Keep any leftover cake refrigerated.

99. CHOCOLATE CAKE

Prep Time: 15 Minutes | Cook Time: Hour

Total Time: 1 Hour 15 Minutes | Serving: 8

Ingredients

- ◆ 3 large Eggs
- ◆ a dash of Salt
- ◆ 2 cups of All Purpose Flour
- ◆ 1 and a half cups of Milk
- ◆ 1 and a half cups of Sugar
- ◆ 1 tsp Baking Powder
- ◆ 1 cup of Coco Powder
- ◆ 1 tsp Vanilla Essence, Use vanilla sugar if vanilla essence is unavailable
- ◆ 250 Grams Butter, use margarine if you prefer

Chocolate Topping:

- ◆ 50 grams of unsalted butter
- ◆ 500 grams cooking chocolate
- ◆ 1 cup of cooking cream or whipping cream

Instructions

1. Put all of the dry ingredients in a big basin and sift them together.
2. Put the sugar in a big bowl for mixing. Melt the butter slowly while stirring all the time.
3. When the sugar and butter are combined, mix until the sugar is dissolved.
4. Whisk in eggs until they become frothy. Add vanilla sugar or vanilla essence.
5. Mix in all of the dry ingredients, whisking constantly. Blend in milk until it's smooth.
6. The rice cooker's bottom and sides should be greased. Apply butter! It makes the cake taste better.) Transfer the mixture to the rice cooker. You are ready to go after you press Start.

Chocolate Topping Method:

1. A bowl that fits tightly over the top of your pot is required.
2. Split the chocolate into tiny fragments and transfer it to a tiny basin.
3. Place the bowl containing the chocolate over a pot of boiling water. Add the butter and cream and mix thoroughly once the chocolate has softened. Ideally, your bowl should fit halfway within the pot, touching the hot water but not the bottom.

100. RICE COOKER PANCAKES

Prep Time: 10 Minutes | Cook Time: 1 Hour 5 Minutes

Total Time: 1 Hour 15 Minutes | Serving: 8

Ingredients

- 1 tsp vanilla
- 1 1/2 cup of 2% milk
- 2 cups of flour
- 2.5 tbsp white sugar
- 2 eggs
- 2 1/2 tsp baking powder
- 1/4 tsp salt

Instructions

1. In a big mixing dish, mix the dry ingredients (flour, baking powder, and salt). Mix everything together.
2. The wet ingredients should be measured, blended, and mixed thoroughly.
3. Stirring as you pour, add the wet ingredients to the dry ingredients. Mix until the batter is completely mixed and there are no visible lumps.
4. Apply cooking spray to the inside pot of the rice cooker, being sure to cover the entire surface. Pour in the batter, taking care to keep it from burning on the sides.
5. Choose "cake" on your fuzzy logic rice cooker if you have one. Check the cooking directions in the following guidelines if your rice cooker is manual.
6. Once cooked, remove the lid and let the pancake cool for five minutes. Remove with caution, following the aforementioned guidelines.
7. Slice a cake as you would a cake and serve with your preferred toppings.

101. RICE COOKER PANDAN CHIFFON CAKE

Prep Time: 20 Minutes | Cook Time: 50 Minutes

Total Time: 1 Hour 10 Minutes | Serving: 8

Ingredients

DRY:

- 40 grams Sugar
- 100 grams Cake Flour
- ¼ tsp Himalayan Pink Salt or Kosher Salt
- 1 tsp Baking Powder

WET:

- 40 grams Coconut Milk
- 30 ml Pandan Juice (5 Fresh Pandan leaves blended with ¼ cup of Water and strain – use 30 ml of that Pandan Juice)
- 4 Egg Yolks
- 50 grams Coconut Oil

Other:

- 40 grams Sugar
- ½ tsp Cream of Tartar
- 4 Egg Whites

Instructions

1. Blend ¼ cup of water with five fresh or frozen pandan leaves.
2. Reserve 30 ml for the recipe after straining.
3. As an alternative, combine 30 ml of water with 1 tsp of pandan extract.
4. Combine four egg yolks with 40 grams of Sugar. Mix in 50 grams of coconut oil and ¼ tsp of salt. Mix in the coconut milk and pandan juice.
5. Mix thoroughly after adding the baking powder and cake flour after sieving. Whisk the egg whites in another dish until frothy. Whisk in the cream of tartar.
6. Add the Sugar gradually while stirring. Once your egg whites are nice and stiff, keep whisking.
7. One tbsp at a time, gently fold the egg whites into the other wet ingredients. Use coconut oil to spritz or grease the rice cooker pot. To get rid of the air bubbles, tilt your pot a few times. Take advantage of your rice cooker's "cake" mode.

102. RICE COOKER CHOCOLATE CAKE

Prep Time: 5 Minutes | Cook Time: 1 Hour

Total Time: 1 Hour 5 Minutes | Serving: 12

Ingredients

- 1 tsp baking soda
- 1 1/2 cups of white flour
- 1 tbsp vinegar
- 90 ml sunflower oil
- 1 cup of water
- 1/2 tsp salt

- 1/2 tsp vanilla
- 1/2 tsp cinnamon
- 1/4 tsp double-acting baking powder
- 1/2 cup of raw sugar (or just white sugar)
- 4 tbsp dark cocoa

Instructions

1. Stir the dry ingredients together 1/2 cup of raw sugar, four tbsp powdered dark chocolate, 1/2 cup of white flour, 1/4 tsp double-acting baking powder (omit for thicker cake), v1/2 tsp baking soda, and 1 are the ingredients for 1.5 cups of white flour.
2. Thoroughly combine the dry ingredients.
3. Stir in wet components 90 milliliters of sunflower oil (you may use any kind), one tbsp of vinegar, half a tsp of vanilla, and one cup of water.
4. Mix thoroughly for one minute, being careful not to overwork the batter.
5. After greasing the rice cooker bowl, pour batter into it.
6. If your rice cooker does not have a slow option, don't panic. Just set it to "slow" and cook for 60 minutes.
7. Certain rice cookers switch to the warm cycle after five minutes, let the cooker run in that mode for a few minutes (similar to preheating), and then reset the timer for the remaining time, making the total cook time sixty minutes. After 45 minutes, check the cake. The cake is done when a toothpick inserted into the center and along the edges comes out clean.
8. When the cake is done, remove the rice cooker bowl from the machine and let it cool in the bowl for fifteen minutes before taking it out.
9. Place a flat plate on top of the rice cooker bowl and smoothly invert the dish to remove the cake. Dust with icing sugar or cover with your preferred frosting.
10. Aim to consume only part of the cake in one sitting!

103. BANANA CAKE IN RICE COOKER

Prep Time: 30 Minutes | Cook Time: 1 Hour

Total Time: 1 Hour 30 Minutes | Serving: 8

Ingredients

Wet ingredients:

- 100 gram (3.5 ounce) unsalted butter, melted
- 1 tsp vanilla extract
- 100 gram (1/2 cup) sugar
- 2 ripe bananas pureed with a food processor/blender
- 4 large size eggs, separate the whites from the yolks

Dry ingredients:

- ⅛ tsp salt (omit if you are using salted butter)
- 1 cup of (120 gram, or 4 1/4 ounce) all-purpose flour, sifted
- 1 tsp baking powder

Tools:

- 1 food processor/blender
- 1 whisk, either a hand-held one or an electric mixer with a whisk attachment
- 1 rice cooker

Instructions

1. There's no need to grease and flour if the pot in your rice cooker has a Teflon non-stick coating. If not, kindly flour and butter the saucepan very lightly.
2. Beat the egg whites in a large mixing bowl until they reach a medium peak, adding the sugar in three batches as you go.
3. Next, incorporate the melted butter, pureed banana, egg yolks, and vanilla extract into the egg whites. Thoroughly combine each component before adding the next.
4. Using a spatula, gently incorporate the dry ingredients—all-purpose flour, baking powder, and salt—into the wet ingredients. To avoid collapsing the airy batter, stop once the dry ingredients are combined.
5. Transfer the batter to the pot of the rice cooker and set it inside. Activate the "cook" button. Wait for ten minutes after it reaches "warm" temperature. For a total of four cycles of "cook" and "warm," repeat the "cook" and "warm" cycle three more times.
6. When the rice cooker lid is open, check to see if the cake is made by using a cake tester. Continue the cycle of "cook" and "warm" until the cake is done if it's still not cooked.
7. The banana cake should fall onto the plate with ease once you remove the pot from the rice cooker and cover it with a plate that is wider than the opening. After slicing the cake, proceed to serve it.

104. RICE COOKER UPSIDE DOWN CAKE

Prep Time: 10 Minutes | Cook Time: 5 Minutes | Additional Time: 1 Hour 5 Minutes

Total Time: 1 Hour 20 Minutes | Serving: 8

Ingredients

FRUIT COMPOTE:

- 1/4 cup of white sugar
- 5 small plums
- 1 Tbsp butter

BATTER:

- 2/3 cup of sour cream
- 1/4 tsp salt
- 1 tsp baking powder
- 1 stick butter
- 1 tsp vanilla extract
- 1 cup of flour (all purpose)
- 1/2 cup of sugar
- 1/2 tsp baking soda
- 1 egg

Instructions

1. Prepare the fruit compote:
2. Each plum should be cleaned and cut into wedges that are 0.5 inches thick.
3. Turn the heat up to medium-high in a pan. Put in one tbsp of butter. Add 1/4 cup of sugar and the plum wedges once it has melted. Mix everything together.
4. Cook, stirring occasionally, until the sugar dissolves, the plum is cooked, and the juices have reduced to a thick syrup, about 8 to 10 minutes. Take off the heat and let it cool down sufficiently to handle.

Batter:

1. In a dish, mix all dry ingredients and whisk to blend. With a mixer or high-sided bowl, combine the remaining butter and 1/2 cup of sugar; beat until creamy.
2. Stir the sour cream, egg, and vanilla together with the remaining wet ingredients.
3. Carefully stir in the sour cream mixture after creaming the butter. Once blended, stir the dry components into the wet mixture.

Place in the rice cooker:

1. Make sure you use a circle of parchment paper to line the bottom of your rice cooker.
2. Arrange the plum wedges in a spiral on top of the paper circle at the bottom of the pot. Any leftover liquids should be equally spooned over the plums.
3. Apply cooking oil spray to lightly coat the circle. Using a spatula, pour the batter over the plums, covering them fully. Once the rice cooker is closed, select the "Cake" preset.
4. After cooking, let it cool until you can remove it with ease. Refer to the directions above for advice on how to remove with ease!

105. CALAMANSI YOGHURT CAKE

Prep Time: 30 Minutes | Cook Time: 1 Hour

Total Time: 1 Hour 30 Minutes | Serving: 8

Ingredients

- 150 gram plain yoghurt
- 4 eggs, separate egg whites from egg yolks
- 1/3 cup of canola oil
- 3 tbsp calamansi juice
- 1/2 cup of sugar
- Dry ingredients:
- 1/8 tsp salt
- 1 cup of all purpose flour, sifted
- 1 tsp baking powder

Tools:

- 1 rice cooker
- 1 whisk

Instructions

1. Beat the egg whites in a mixing dish until they reach a medium peak. Gradually add the sugar, working in batches (I generally do this in three). Whisk in the egg yolks after that.
2. Yogurt and canola oil should be whisked together in another bowl until creamy. Pour this mixture into the eggs and stir well.
3. Apply a spatula and fold the dry ingredients into the wet ingredients. Just make sure that everything is thoroughly mixed; don't overdo this step to ruin all of your hard work aerating the egg whites. Add the calamansi juice last and thoroughly combine.
4. (Details optional) To make it easier to remove the completed cake from the rice cooker pot, lightly coat the pot with oil or melted butter. You can omit this step if your pot is coated in Teflon.
5. Fill the rice cooker pot with the batter. Press the "cook" button after inserting the rice cooker pot into the appliance. After it becomes "warm," give it ten minutes. For a total of four "cook" and "warm" cycles, repeat the "cook" and "warm" procedure three more times.
6. Take the lid from the rice cooker and use a toothpick to check the doneness of the cake. It's finished if the toothpick emerges clean. If not, continue the cycle of "cook" and "warm" until the cake is done.
7. The cake should fall onto the plate after removing the rice cooker pot and covering it with a plate that is broader than the aperture. After allowing the cake to cool somewhat on a wire rack, serve it at room temperature.

106. PANDAN RICE COOKER SPONGE CAKE

Prep Time: 30 Minutes | Cook Time: 40 Minutes

Total Time: 1 Hour 10 Minutes | Serving: 12

Ingredients

- 50 g corn oil or other vegetable oil
- 120 g low protein flour cake flour
- 80 ml milk
- 15 g pandan leaves
- 1 tsp baking powder
- 4 eggs grade A
- 120 g fine granulated sugar

Instructions

1. Grease the inside pot of the rice cooker lightly (if the bottom burns or isn't non-stick, line it with parchment paper).
2. Sift through a sieve after combining cake flour and baking powder.
3. After measuring out 70 ml of pandan milk, blend the milk and pandan leaves till very fine. In a mixing dish, combine eggs and sugar; whisk to thoroughly combine.
4. To make 45°C/113°F warm water, put 1000 ml of water and 400 ml of hot water in a large steel basin.
5. Immerse the mixing bowl in a warm water bath; whisk the egg mixture at medium speed until it begins to thicken; drop the speed to low and whisk until stiff (the egg mixture will form ribbons that will remain on top for some time before gently dissolving).
6. In a separate mixing bowl, mix together corn oil, pandan milk, and half of the flour until well combined. Add ⅓ of the beaten eggs and stir to incorporate. Mix until smooth after adding the remaining flour.
7. In two batches, add the remaining beaten eggs and gently stir with a hand whisk.
8. Gently fold with a spatula until thoroughly combined, then tap several times on the countertop to release big air bubbles.
9. Pour batter into the inner pot of the rice cooker and tap again to release any big bubbles.
10. Once a wooden stick in the center comes out clean, cook it for 40 minutes in the rice cooker. I use the "Quick Cook" setting; it takes around 40 minutes for each cycle. You must press the "Cook" button several times until the cake is thoroughly cooked if your rice cooker shifts to "Keep Warm" before it is finished cooking. Different rice cookers operate in different ways.
11. After turning the rice cooker sponge cake over onto a wire rack, let it cool for ten to fifteen minutes.

107. HONEY GLAZED UPSIDE DOWN APPLE CAKE

Prep Time: 30 Minutes | Cook Time: 1 Hour

Total Time: 1 Hour 30 Minutes | Serving: 8

Ingredients

Apple slices and juice:

- 1 apple (I used a Fuji apple)
- 1 cinnamon stick
- 2 tbsp honey

Wet ingredients:

- 50 gram butter, melted
- 1/4 cup of sugar
- 1/4 cup of milk
- 4 eggs, separate the whites from the yolks
- 1 tsp vanilla essence

Dry ingredients:

- 1/8 tsp salt
- 1 cup of all purpose flour, sifted
- 1 tsp baking powder

Tools:

- 1 rice cooker
- 1 whisk

Instructions

1. Apple cored and peeled; divided into sixteen pieces. Put the apple, stick of cinnamon, and honey in a skillet and heat over low heat until the honey bursts. When the apple is tender but still firm, remove from the fire and leave aside to allow the apples to absorb the delicious liquid as you finish preparing the cake.
2. Beat the egg whites in a mixing dish until they reach a medium peak. Gradually add the sugar, working in batches (I generally do this in three).
3. Next, mix the egg whites with the egg yolks, milk, melted butter, and vanilla extract. Blend each ingredient thoroughly before adding the next.

4. Finally, use a spatula to incorporate the dry ingredients into the wet components. Just make sure that everything is thoroughly mixed; don't overdo this step to ruin all of your hard work aerating the egg whites.

5. Save the cooking liquid to glaze the cake after you've placed the apple sections in the bottom of your rice cooker pot. Fill the pot with enough batter to submerge the apples completely.

6. Press the "cook" button after inserting the rice cooker pot into the appliance. After it becomes "warm," give it ten minutes. For a total of four "cook" and "warm" cycles, repeat the "cook" and "warm" procedure three more times.

7. Open the lid from the rice cooker and use a toothpick to check the doneness of the cake. It's finished if the toothpick emerges clean. If not, continue the cycle of "cook" and "warm" until the cake is done.

8. The cake should fall onto the plate after removing the rice cooker pot and covering it with a plate that is broader than the aperture.

9. Use the cooking liquid that was set aside after the apples were cooked to lightly brush the cake's top. This will make the cake look glossy, but more significantly, it will keep its moisture content until the next day, assuming it survives that long.

108. RICE COOKER MOCHA CASTELLA CAKE

Prep Time: 20 Minutes | Cook Time: 50 Minutes

Total Time: 1 Hour 10 Minutes | Serving: 6

Ingredients

- ½ cup of sugar
- 1 tsp instant coffee powder
- ¼ cup of all purpose flour
- 1 tbsp vegetable oil
- 4 egg whites at room temperature
- 1tsp cocoa powder
- 1tbsp milk warmed
- 1tsp vanilla extract
- 5 egg yolks

Instructions

1. After dissolving the instant coffee powder in the heated milk, stir in the vanilla extract and vegetable oil.

2. Whisk the egg whites in another basin and gradually add the sugar in three parts until a stiff meringue forms. One egg yolk at a time, gradually add them while whisking to make a firm meringue.

3. Using a rubber spatula, fold or mix the batter until it is thoroughly combined after sifting the flour and cocoa powder into the dish.

4. After applying oil or cold butter to the inside of the rice cooker, pour in the batter. Use a chopstick to stir out any large air bubbles.

5. In the rice cooker, cook the batter for 50 minutes or until it is thoroughly cooked. After cooling, serve. Have fun!

109. BLUEBERRY CHEESECAKE IN A RICE COOKER

Prep Time: 10 Minutes | Cook Time: 1 Hour 30 Minutes

Total Time: 1 Hour 40 Minutes | Serving: 6

Ingredients

- ¼ lemon juice/essence
- Extra sugar
- 3 tbs margarine
- 2 eggs
- 1 cup of blue berries
- 4 tbs flour
- 200g cream cheese
- 200mL heavy cream
- 80g sugar
- 100g Marie biscuits
- ½ cup of water

Instructions

1. Remove the heavy cream and eggs from the refrigerator. After that, place the Marie biscuits in a ziplock bag and pound them until they are finely chopped.
2. In the microwave, warm the margarine for 40 seconds. Stir in until the mixture comes together after adding the crushed biscuits.
3. Transfer the biscuit mixture and margarine to the bowl of the rice cooker. Next, shape the biscuit base by pressing it down from the top using cling film. To set, place in the refrigerator.
4. Reduce the size of the cream cheese and place it in a bowl. Microwave for one minute or until it becomes soft. Blend until silky.
5. Mix the cheese after sifting in the sugar. After that, mix some more after sifting in the flour. Before adding the eggs to the mixture, stir them. Stir in the lemon essence and heavy cream.
6. After adding the ingredients, allow it to settle over the biscuit base. After that, put the rice cooker's bowl inside and turn it on.
7. Examine whether the cake comes loose at the corners after the first rice cycle is finished. Additionally, use a skewer to see if the center is done. If not, begin as many rice cycles as necessary (two cycles were required in my instance).
8. After finishing, let the bowl cool to room temperature. After that, refrigerate the cake.
9. Get two plates ready. After turning the cheesecake over onto a plate, move it to a serving plate.
10. If you have fresh or frozen blueberries, wash them or allow them to defrost. Place in a saucepan with a little sugar and cook over low heat until they become tender.
11. Top the cheesecake with the blueberries, cover, and chill until ready to serve.

110. RICE COOKER RICE CAKES

Prep Time: 10 Minutes | Cook Time: 20 Minutes

Total Time: 30 Minutes | Serving: 4

Ingredients

- 2 cups of jasmine rice
- 1/4 tsp salt
- 4 cups of water

Tools:

- rice cooker
- loaf pan
- saran plastic wrap

Instructions

1. After washing, drain the rice. Next, put the rice, water, and salt in a rice cooker and simmer until the rice cooker indicates "warm" temperature.
2. Lift the lid, then press and fluff the rice using a spatula or the rice paddle (which is typically included with your rice cooker). Compared to regular steamed rice, the cooked rice used to make rice cakes should be substantially wetter.
3. Use saran plastic wrap to line a loaf pan. Using a rice paddle or spatula, transfer the warm rice to the pan and press it into place. After all of the rice has been transferred, place another piece of saran wrap over the top surface and continue pressing to flatten it.
4. After packing the rice as tightly as possible, make holes for steam to escape by poking the top of plastic wrap with a stick.
5. Allow the rice cake to cool; placing it in the refrigerator will hasten this process.
6. After the rice cake cools fully, take it out of the mold, take off the plastic wrap, and cut it into 1-inch cubes. Accompany with your preferred savory cuisine.